Presented To:

_____

From:

_____

Date:

_____

FILMING
GOD

A JOURNEY FROM
SKEPTICISM TO FAITH

Darren Wilson

DESTINY IMAGE® PUBLISHERS, INC.

P.O. Box 310, Shippensburg, PA 17257-0310

"Speaking to the Purposes of God for This Generation and for the Generations to Come."

This book and all other Destiny Image, Revival Press, MercyPlace, Fresh Bread, Destiny Image Fiction, and Treasure House books are available at Christian bookstores and distributors worldwide.

For a U.S. bookstore nearest you, call 1-800-722-6774.

For more information on foreign distributors, call 717-532-3040.

Reach us on the Internet: www.destinyimage.com.

ISBN 13 Trade Paper: 978-0-7684-3770-6

ISBN 13 Hardcover: 978-0-7684-3771-3

ISBN 13 Large Print: 978-0-7684-3772-0

ISBN 13 E-book: 978-0-7684-8999-6

For Worldwide Distribution, Printed in the U.S.A.

1 2 3 4 5 6 7 / 15 14 13 12 11

Dedication

Dedicated to my children, Serenity, Stryder, and River. My hope and prayer is that you will never have to go through as much as your father did to believe in a God of extravagant love and wonders. I also pray that you will experience much more than your dad has or ever will, and that you will be a light to a darkened world.

Acknowledgments

There are a lot of people to thank for a book like this, far too many than can be listed here. First and foremost, though, I want to thank my wife, Jenell, for being the reason this book (and my movies) even exist. You pushed and prodded your spiritually dead husband back to life. You never gave up, and you never took no for an answer. Without your love, support, and spiritual tenacity, I would not be the man I am today, this book would not exist, my movies would be figments of God's imagination, and millions of people around the world would not have been changed. Thank you, my dear.

Also, to my parents, Gary and Linda, my first fans! It's been a long, hard road to get here, but we finally made it. Thank you for never giving up on your dreaming son, for always allowing me to chase after those dreams, and for being the consummate support system for a starry-eyed kid. You are the best parents in the world (Dad, don't let it go to your head, though).

Endorsements

The Bible is filled with challenging paradoxes, like in Psalm 2:11, *"rejoice with trembling."* Fear and joy don't fit together too well in my thinking. But apparently they do with God. And that is how I see *Filming God*. I don't remember the last time I had so much fun reading a manuscript, while at the same time being so challenged about my own life. As I write this endorsement, my heart is filled with both joy and sober mindedness. Strangely, they go well together. Darren Wilson writes as he talks—very honest and upfront, almost raw, yet inviting and extremely insightful. I found myself laughing out loud, saying to my wife, "You've got to hear this," and yet in the next moment, reexamining my own journey with God. I believe this book will be used to influence many to simply trust God beyond reason. It will be the most intelligent thing we'll ever do.

BILL JOHNSON
Pastor, Bethel Church
Author, *When Heaven Invades Earth*
and *Dreaming With God*

I love Darren's story because he is so blatantly honest. The greatest skeptic will believe him as he deals with angels, miracles, and outrageous God exploits. Tighten your seat belt and get ready for an amazing God adventure that will expand your vision of God.

Sid Roth, Host

It's Supernatural! Television

www.SidRoth.org

They say to "never judge a book by its cover." But sometimes I read a book just because I love its cover, and in this case, its author. I love Darren Wilson. He is like my long lost brother. Darren's passion for the things of God is contagious through his films and now through his book, *Filming God*. I love this book, and I think you will too.

Philip Mantofa

Pastor, Mawar Sharon Church

Surabaya, Indonesia

Darren Wilson's book, *Filming God*, is outstanding. What I love most about both Darren and this book, is that both represent "realness." *Filming God* will stir you and help you to believe that the Lord can do anything through you if you simply yield to His purposes. Darren paints a beautiful, clear picture of his journey into filming God's stories—and I love his humor too.

Patricia King

www.XPmedia.com

I just finished reading Darren Wilson's *Filming God*. Darren's story was captivating. It is an easy read, but don't let the simplicity of his style of storytelling fool you. He has also dealt with heavy theological issues in this book. It is an exciting read because Darren invites you in to see and understand how he, a self-acclaimed skeptic, becomes the director of two full length films that display the miraculous power of God, *The Finger of God;* and the great love of God, *Furious Love.* I recommend you buy and read this book and then give it to your friends to read. I plan on having it in our bookstore and available at our schools throughout the world. *Filming God* is an amazing book about an amazing God who has made normal people into amazing people. In the midst of the storytelling are insights into the amazing people's lives and the cost of having divine Spirit empower human flesh.

RANDY CLARK
www.randyclarkministries.org

Now there are also many other things that Jesus did. Were every one of them to be written, I suppose that the world itself could not contain the books that would be written (John 21:25).

Contents

Foreword

I'm sitting in my home in Connecticut with my wife Jessica and my son Ocean Alexander when the phone rings. The lady on the other end of the phone says, "There is a gentleman named Darren Wilson who wants to film a documentary about people getting touched by the power of God and seeing legitimate signs and wonders."

She says, "He has recently been touched by God for the first time in a very powerful way. In an angelic experience he was told to make a film of God moving and that he was to document it for the world to see."

She also tells me she told him, "You need to talk to Jason and Jessica Westerfield in Connecticut by Yale University because there is nobody better that I know who is a close friend with God, has incredible miracles, signs and wonders, and has a passion for the film and entertainment industry."

I was humbled by what she had said about our family and asked her if there was anything else I should know.

She said, "You should be expecting a phone call!"

It wasn't long after that my phone rang with Darren Wilson on the other end greeting me in a warm and sincere way. Darren shared with me about what had happened with him in His encounter and about his spiritual background. Darren hadn't had anything supernatural happen in his life prior to his encounter. He shared with me the evolution of his film project and that his heart's desire was to please Jesus and be obedient. Darren was stepping out on a limb and trusting God to do something that only God could do.

We set up a date and time to film and soon Darren was arriving at the New Haven airport for us to pick him up. That night we recognized Darren was exhausted from traveling all over the world. He had been getting interviews from numerous people in many countries that had incredible stories. We took Darren out to eat that night at a very nice place to bless him and be as generous and hospitable as we could. That night Darren stayed on our couch in our little apartment at the time.

The Lord spoke to me, "Darren needs rest, so take really good care of him. He thinks he is here to film, but I also want to personally refresh him and bless him."

That morning Jessica made a delicious breakfast and we had a great time in conversation. After breakfast I went to rest and pray on the same couch Darren was sleeping on. I was happy to see Darren vibrant and getting excited for what was going to happen next.

The Lord spoke to me, "Go to Yale University. Once there, I will speak to you and direct you. Many lives will get touched supernaturally by My Spirit and My love. I am with you, get up now and go." I got up from the couch and shared with Darren and my wife what the Lord had just shared with me and then we were off to Yale University.

As we walked around Yale in the freshman dorms court-yard, I noticed a group of people standing around. The Holy

Spirit spoke to me and said, "Go over there and I will lead you from there."

I told Darren this and he said, "You mean you don't have anything yet, and we are just going to go over there?" He looked a little nervous and curious at the same time.

I told him, "This is sometimes how my relationship and friendship with God is, and I have to trust Him and not try to figure everything out, but He always shows up!"

When we arrived to the group, I made small talk until God began to speak to me, then I shared with numerous individuals what God had to say about them. The Holy Spirit came with His power and presence and people were tearing up crying. Miracles of physical and emotional healing took place when revelation knowledge was spoken, without anybody touching each other. When detailed information was revealed about each person's life, the group was really intrigued and drawn in as they knew there was no way I could have known what I was telling them about their lives.

The Lord had me pray for the wind to begin to blow over the creation in the courtyard and for the angels to come. As I prayed, God did incredible wondrous signs, and the winds began to blow over all the trees where we were as the presence of God got thicker and heavier. The group was standing in awe of what they were witnessing and experiencing with their own eyes. We were able to share about the cross Jesus died on for humanity's sins and the Gospel of the Kingdom. People got saved, healed, delivered, and filled with the Holy Spirit. It was incredible as the heavens opened over the whole courtyard area.

Darren was blown away from what he had just encountered and didn't have a paradigm or mental box for it. I told him, "That's the Kingdom coming on earth as it is in Heaven, and the Lord's prayer being answered. God was pouring out His Spirit on all flesh and unconditionally loving people."

Later that day, we witnessed many more miracles. One man on crutches was healed of broken bones in his leg as witnessed on the film *Finger of God*. This miracle took place on the set production where they happened to be filming the latest Indiana Jones movie *Crystal Skull*. I thought that it was interesting that two films were being filmed on the same location that day; one by Steven Spielberg and George Lucas with Harrison Ford and one with Darren Wilson and Jason Westerfield. As much as I liked the high quality and special effects of *Crystal Skull*, I liked God's film better because it was real, eternal, and lives were changed forever!

Darren Wilson is an amazing man with a heart after God. He has a wonderful wife and children that make up the rest of the cast of his real life story. God is using him in incredible ways to introduce those inside the church and outside of the church to His incredible power and love for humankind through making movies. Filming God's glory manifesting is the greatest thing in the world to film and such a privilege to be part of. As you read through this book, *Filming God*, may you be drawn to our Creator and Lover, the Lord Jesus, and go forth becoming a compassionate ambassador of His Kingdom of light and love.

JASON T. WESTERFIELD
Founder and President of Kingdom Reality
www.Kingdomreality.com

Introduction

I never wanted to be a spiritual lightning rod. I don't particularly like the extreme right or the extreme left. Radicals make me nervous. I feel just as comfortable in a Catholic church as I do in a Charismatic one. I like things around me to be fairly safe, even keeled—normal.

But a funny thing tends to happen when you hand your life over to God, no questions asked. He takes what you thought you wanted and shows you something better—something so much infinitely better that you can only marvel at how simple-minded your past dreams were.

I come from a "normal" church background, and by normal I mean nothing ever really happened at church other than, well, church. I was raised in a Baptist environment, which is about as middle as you can get in evangelical Christianity.

The God I grew up with was a God who was very normal, very steady, and who always, always, always made sense. But it wasn't just that He made sense; it was that somehow, some way, we could figure out what that sense was. He was not a God who did strange things and then didn't explain Himself. He was rational, intelligent, and pragmatic. When God did something, it was like a Swiss train: reliable and always on time. He was a God who loved me, certainly, but also a God who had a purpose for me; and it was His highest aim to get me to buy into that purpose—not because I loved Him, but mostly because it was His will that I do so. That phrase would grow to haunt me in my teenage years and on into college. *His will.* It was the most terrifying concept in the world to me.

I often encounter this issue with my students. I teach at Judson University, an American Baptist school just outside of Chicago, and each year I get a new crop of students who are subjected to the very same stories you are about to encounter on the following pages. They realize two things very early on: 1) that I am as sane as they are; and 2) that I am not in the least bit interested if they believe me or not.

TELLING THE TRUTH

It is much easier to be called a liar when you know you are telling the truth. I know my students can live healthy, productive, fruitful lives for God even if they don't believe in the limitless God I tell them about. This was a lesson my friend Jason Westerfield taught me. Jason is a lover of God who walks in the supernatural like few people I have met. I was sitting in a hotel room with him in Salem, Massachusetts, lamenting on the various emails I was getting from fundamentalist Christians decrying my film, *Finger of God,* as horse manure, and I was wishing the more conservative church would "wake up" and start living in the power of Christ.

Jason (who, mind you, is one of the most power-filled Christians I know) looked at me and gently but firmly put me in my place. He reminded me that I should be careful about what I say about God's children. The more conservative brothers and sisters have done many things for the Kingdom and have led countless millions to the Lord. Whether or not they believe my movies or me does not make them less important to the Kingdom. It may make things harder for them than they need to be, but at the core, we are one and the same. After all, as long as we all love and serve and trust Jesus, we're on the same team.

Of course, after years of teaching on the college level at a Christian university, one thing has become unmistakably clear. The vast majority of my Christian students love and serve God. But very few of them trust Him very much.

I understand their mindset, because for most of my life I was steeped in it. I knew God loved me, but I didn't for an instant think that He was looking out for my best interest. At best, He would maybe allow me to continue doing what I loved on the side while I spent the majority of my time doing whatever it was He wanted me to do for Him. I believed He loved me, but mostly I believed He just wanted to use me. So I fought battles with Him. I knew He wanted me to give everything over to Him, that He wanted me to "lay my life at His feet" and tell Him He could do whatever He wanted with me.

But like so many other evangelical Christians, I was afraid that He would "send me to Africa" or something equally horrendous. He was going to ask me to stop writing and start serving in a food camp somewhere. Or He was going to make me become a missionary. I wouldn't be able to watch sports anymore because I wouldn't get cable television in the jungle. I wouldn't have a comfortable bed. I wouldn't have a nice home. I wouldn't have any money at all.

This is just plain stupid.

It took two things to set me straight. One was a powerful encounter with the living God (you'll read about that soon). The other was having children of my own. This way of thinking—that God is at best a loving tyrant who only thinks of Himself and His means—is like thinking that my children live to serve me and me alone. It would be like me saying to my daughter, "I don't care that you like to sing and dance; *accounting* is what I really want you to do, so if you love me, do it, and forget about all that other stuff." In truth, that first phrase, "I don't care," is totally incongruent with a passionately loving God. He *does* care. He cares immensely. That's why He made you the way He did. It's why He gave you the desires and talents that you have.

TRUSTING GOD

So can we trust God? Of course we can. It was only after I gave my creative self (the part of me I cared about the most and held on to the longest) to Him that He not only gave me success but also showed me that He had even *bigger* dreams for me than I could ever have imagined. I had been selling myself short my whole life. God dreams much bigger than we do, which makes *not* trusting Him with our deepest desires even more absurd.

But it is my contention that the church, and particularly the church in the Western world, is drowning in this mania. On U2's album, *No Line on the Horizon*, Bono sings a line that I believe is as prophetic as it is good. In the song, "Stand Up Comedy," he sings, I am certain, to the American church with the line, "Stop helping God across the road like a little old lady...."

I am convinced that the church is not living up to its full potential because the church does not fully believe God is who He says He is. To us, He's a little old lady, quite powerless, fairly hard to talk to, and not someone you want to spend much time with. He's fairly boring, but we put up with Him once a week because it's the right thing to do. Sure we'll go and see Him on Sunday mornings, but when we leave His house, He remains there, waving to us from the door, hoping we'll come back next week.

This was the God I used to serve, but it certainly isn't the God of the Bible, and I think most people know it. I think deep down we all know that God is active, powerful, and operates on a level of existence and knowledge of the inner workings of the universe that is wholly incomprehensible to us. But we're terrified of Him, of who He really might be, not because we are afraid of the truth, but because *we don't trust what that kind of a God will do to us.*

The root of the problem is in our total misunderstanding of love at the God level. Before I encountered the ferocious love that God had for me, my entire understanding of His love was locked away in my brain. It was head knowledge. Of course God loved me; of course He loves the world. He is love. I knew that. It is the first thing we teach our children in Sunday school. The problem with simply *understanding* that God loves us is the emotional disconnect that is built into such an understanding.

Jesus was fond of explaining the love of God for us as that of a bridegroom for his bride. (See John 3:29.) Simply knowing in my head that God loves me would be like living my whole life watching my wife from a distance. I could visit her room, watch her do things, and tell her how much I love her. But "head love," as I call it, is like love that never touches. There is no embrace, only knowledge. I can know everything there is to know about my wife, but what satisfies me the most is when I embrace her. Communication is wonderful, but true love requires a physical connection—a spiritual connection.

Or maybe it's better put this way: on your wedding night, you don't sit around and talk the whole time….

In short, love requires the heart.

GOD ON A HEART LEVEL

The first story details my first real experience with God on a heart level. The stories that follow all have one thing in common, and indeed it is within this truth where the seeds of a spiritual revolution lay. The common thread connecting all of these stories is that God is a God of encounter. The entire Bible is made up of stories about how God invades His creation and interacts with His people. It is not a book of good ideas. It is not a book of impersonal academic instruction. It is a book of raw, human experience as it comes into contact with a delightfully loving, forgiving God. It is the greatest love story ever told.

And as all Christians will agree, the greatest love of all is shown in the person of Jesus Christ. This is God at His best. Throughout the Old Testament, God delivers His people through mighty works, signs, and wonders. He parts a sea. He blinds entire armies. He makes axes float and donkeys talk. But when Jesus hits the scene, the whole game changes. It is as if God was saying at that moment, "Enough already. If these people won't believe My works, then I'll come down there Myself and *show* them how much I love them." Jesus didn't come to write a book; He came to touch the human race. He ate with us. He laughed with us. He cried with us. He endured pain with us. What more does God need to do to prove to us that He is very much interested in dealing with us on more than simply a mind level?

In the end, it all comes down to trust. To pray the most dangerous prayer, the one where we ask God to touch us completely and to *take over*, we must first be willing to trust Him. We must begin to see ourselves not as slaves or hired hands, but as sons and daughters. If the Church is to be the Bride, we must first give ourselves—minds, bodies, and souls—to our bridegroom.

I cannot keep anything from Him. I cannot withhold anything. I must place my entire life in His hands and (here is the key) trust that He will do what is best for me. He *does* have my best interest at heart. He *does* care about my desires and my dreams.

Of course, that doesn't mean that He sometimes won't ask us to do difficult things. Some of the stories that follow will show that clearly. We are at war with a very real enemy who not only hates God but hates us as well because we are His prized possessions. This enemy will stop at nothing to destroy the connection we have with our Bridegroom. But as Paul so eloquently states, "Neither life nor death...can separate us from the love of God" (see Rom. 8:38-39).

It is my sincere hope that the stories that follow will stir you to action. This action is a simple yet terrifying one, and it will most certainly lead to a revolution. The action, quite simply, is to decide once and for all to hand yourself, your heart, and your life over to the God of the universe.

As I have learned, it is one thing to accept that Jesus is Lord. It is quite another thing to tell Him He can do whatever He wants with me once that happens.

Author's Note

These are stories I have either witnessed firsthand or have heard from people I have grown to know and love and who are, in my opinion, credible witnesses. They have nothing to gain from telling me these stories; indeed, some have asked me to not include them in my films. These are not people looking to be famous or have more speaking engagements or their own book deals. These are humble people who love Jesus with all their hearts and who work tirelessly on the front lines of some of the darkest spiritual climates on the planet.

As a filmmaker, it is my job to pick up on a person's motivation—and when you spend any decent amount of time with as many people as I have, motivations become fairly clear. The people whose stories you will read in this book are, in my opinion, some of the most credible simply because they have absolutely nothing to gain. These are stories that were told in the backs of vans, on wobbly trains, in quiet kitchens, and in phone conversations between friends.

Look at it this way. If you were to come to me and tell me a story about how your best friend just miraculously escaped a car crash by supernatural means, you would most likely be convinced of the veracity of your story. Why? Because of *who* the story came from. This is your friend; you trust him or her. The person only told you about this story because he or she thought you would believe it.

Do people lie about the spiritual things that happen to them? Of course they do. Could some of these people be lying to me? I would be naive if I said no. But no one ever told me a story because they thought I might put it in a book. Many times the camera wasn't even rolling. There is little motivation to lie.

That being said, many of the stories you are about to read will seem too incredible to be true. In the end, it is up to you to decide whether or not you believe them or me. I can only report them to you as they were relayed to me, from the mouths of the people who experienced them.

Chapter 1

THE MOST UNLIKELY MAN

All I did was ask for an idea. That's how it started.

I should probably start things off by establishing the scene, the spiritual landscape of my heart for the nearly 30 years prior to heading down this road of trying to film a God who is invisible. I have been called many things since releasing my first feature film, *Finger of God:* a liar, a nut, deceived, a spokesman for the devil. But for people who knew me before I ever made these movies, the most laughable idea wouldn't be some of the things contained within my films, but the simple fact that I, of all people, would be the one making them.

I started teaching full time in 2000 at Judson University in Elgin, Illinois, a short drive from Chicago. This makes me a university professor, which I realize by default means people perceive that I am somewhat intelligent and not completely insane. I grew up in a middle class home in Monroe,

Michigan, just south of Detroit, and my father was a professor of art at the community college there. My grandfather was a pastor and a writer. So my entire life I have been surrounded by intelligent people and smart ideas. Since I was raised in an artist's home, I was taught to think freely for myself, and I learned early on that you don't have to believe something simply because someone standing in a pulpit said so.

I remember going to various Christian summer camps as a teenager and hearing preachers rail against the sin of rock music and movies—how they were tools of the devil. Even at age 13 I thought they were out of their minds, but all my friends seemed to believe them, and I would listen in abject horror as they would tell me days later how they had burned all their tapes and CDs, even their Christian ones!

I knew, even at an early age, that God was probably a lot bigger than petty rules, but the petty rules made things seem so simple, so black and white. People like black and white. A complicated reality gives us headaches.

MORE THAN SPIRITUAL CLICHÉS

Growing up, faith was as much about normalcy as it was about a relationship with God. It was, as I understood it anyway, mostly about being a good person, treating other people well, going to church on a regular basis, making sure I had fairly consistent "quiet times," and…well, that was pretty much it. Faith seemed to be mostly about what I did—or avoided. The relationship part was kind of hazy.

I heard people talk about it all the time, of course, but it was always through some vague spiritual clichés. I was supposed to "give God control," "surrender myself to Him," "give

Him my heart," and "make my life a living sacrifice" to Him. I didn't have a clue what that stuff meant, but I tried my best. Unfortunately, I also proved to be about as much of a hypocrite as a person could be. My relationship with God didn't change my behavior much, although it did make me more afraid to do certain things for fear that I would feel God's wrath.

I loved God, but only to a point. He died for me, yes, and I understood that He loved me, but our relationship, if there was one, felt like a one way street. It was as if I had married someone but could only send letters. I could never see, hear, or feel my Spouse—I just had to be content knowing that He existed...somewhere. And while He could see me as much as He wanted, I could never see Him. Passion was definitely not part of the picture. I was devoted to Him, for sure. But my love felt more like a really strong *like*. In truth, I'd never really met God, at least not outside of my head, and this fact clouded my thoughts and my faith completely.

But then I started hearing stories.

The next chapter deals more with these stories and my own personal encounter with God, but it should be noted that my first thought upon hearing what God may or may not be doing around the world was one of distrust and skepticism. I'm a professor, so everything I encounter has to pass through my brain first, and that's usually where it stops. I rarely let anything go straight to my heart, because I've seen too many crazy people and heard too many crazy things to just believe whatever I hear. I had learned that it was OK to question the preacher—he was fallible too. Usually my questions about these "God occurrences" would never get answered, and the radical story or teaching would be rejected because it wasn't "normal."

A HEALTHY SKEPTIC

If you were to ask me then (and my wife often did), I would have told you that I was a healthy skeptic. In truth, I didn't believe most of what I heard from other people. It's not that I thought they were lying, I just figured they were embellishing things, remembering poorly, or stretching the truth (sometimes quite a bit). Usually they had something to gain if I believed them. Maybe I'd give them money, support their ministry, stroke their ego, or allow them to keep speaking at other churches. I was sure God *could* do great things, I just didn't think He *did* do them all that much.

After all, most churches in the world were really normal, and they didn't have these things happening on Sunday mornings. At least, they weren't happening at *my* church on Sunday mornings. I guess I couldn't really speak for the other ones. But I thought I could.

In my mind, I was a healthy skeptic, but in reality, I was an impostor. I hid behind my skepticism and called it discernment. But what I have discovered in years of traveling the world filming this stuff, and in dealing with people's opinions of me and my movies, is that skepticism and discernment are two totally different things. Jesus never told us to be skeptical, but instead to be *"wise as serpents and innocent as doves"* (Matt. 10:16). The disciple Thomas simply refused to believe his friends, refused to believe that the impossible thing they were telling him was the truth, and Jesus gently scolded him for it (see John 20:27).

The problem, of course, is that there are so many charlatans out there, so many religious men and women who have been caught lying to us. So many leaders have proven to be hypocrites on a grand scale, and it has become increasingly difficult to trust and believe anything at face value anymore. I don't see this problem going away any time soon, and I think it's both healthy and important that we continue to wrestle with these things, test them, and turn a discerning eye toward them.

What we must *not* do, though, is what I did for 30 years. We must not hide behind our skepticism as an excuse not to go after what God is doing in this day and age. I didn't *want* to believe the things I was hearing, because if they were true, then the whole game changed. I would have a very difficult choice to make. If it was true that God really was moving at an unprecedented rate around the world, and His spirit was doing things that were, well, of biblical proportions on a pretty regular basis, then church for church's sake wasn't going to cut it anymore.

With knowledge comes responsibility, and if I really believed something to be true, that meant I would have to act on that belief or be a hypocrite in the strongest sense of the word. I'd be a Pharisee. I'd be someone who read the Bible and said the right words, but didn't join in the battle. I'd be lukewarm. I'd be God's vomit (see Rev. 3:16).

Let me give my definition of a true skeptic, because I think it's important that you understand my terms. A skeptic is someone who lives in a basic state of fear of the abnormal. You know you're a skeptic if, when you hear about God doing something that may seem a little weird to you, you immediately *look* for a reason to dismiss it. Discernment is different because it implies that what you are encountering *may* be of God. Skeptics look for reasons why it isn't God from the outset. Of course, you may disagree with my definition of a skeptic, but at that point we're dealing with semantics. At least now we are on a proper grounding of what exactly I'm talking about.

I have a much higher tolerance for the "strange" now than I ever did, simply because I've seen so much with my own eyes. But I still try to weigh everything and every person I encounter with a biblical eye. I'm still a professor, I still question everything I hear (even from my most credible sources), and I will be the first person to admit that someone might be lying to me when I interview them. In reality, I can never really know for sure, but having been around enough people and having heard enough stories, you start to get a feel for the authentic after a while. I don't interview anyone who approaches me to do so. I am constantly weighing motives. I work almost entirely on referral—meaning the people I film are brought to my attention by people around the world I trust. At this point, I'd be pretty confident in saying that only the really good con men could make it into my films, simply because of the nature of the people who are referring me to my subjects.

IN THE BIBLE

Perhaps the greatest argument I hear against the things I've seen and film is that "they aren't in the Bible." My friend, Kris Vallotton, a pastor at Bethel Church in Redding, California, is fond of saying, "All of the Bible is in the Kingdom, but not all of the Kingdom is in the Bible." It is true; a story about people getting gold teeth in church isn't in the Bible, but neither is cancer. If someone can prove they were healed of cancer through miraculous means (I know many who can), but it isn't in the Bible, does that mean it didn't really happen? Does that mean the devil did it?

I find it amazing how easy it is for people to credit the devil with so much miraculous power, yet in effect they cannot for a second believe that God is a God of power and strength and mercy and miracles. Certain miraculous occurrences may not be in the Bible, but the Bible is full of miraculous occurrences! Are we going to limit God to only being able to do the types of miracles that He wrote down? The last verse in the Gospels, John 21:25, teases us with this:

> *Now there are also many other things that Jesus did. Were every one of them to be written, I suppose that the world itself could not contain the books that would be written.*

One of my first orders of business upon getting to Heaven is to raid the heavenly library and start finding out exactly what else Jesus did here on earth.

Everyone has their own path to follow, their own race to run. I often see well-meaning Christians trying to hurry certain people forward in their belief systems, even though the person they are trying to hurry clearly isn't yet ready to jump into a limitless Christianity with both feet. All throughout my 20s, I endured pressure from my increasingly believing family to believe these things they were telling me. But I couldn't. I was terrified of believing them. I didn't want to believe. I was comfortable. Content. It was much safer that way.

LESSONS LEARNED

One of the great lessons I learned while making my second film, *Furious Love*, was just how limitless God's patience is. We seem to be in such a hurry to get people to make a decision, sign on the dotted line, admit certain things. But God takes a longer view. He's willing to wait years, sometimes an entire lifetime, to bring us to a place where we will finally yield to His love for us. But that's not the Western way; and in some ways, it doesn't even feel like the Christian way! Yes, we're dealing with life and death here, but my belief won't change simply because you put more pressure on me to believe it. My beliefs will only change when my heart is changed.

God, of course, knew this; and in May 2006, I had an encounter with Him that didn't just change my belief—it changed my heart and destiny forever.

Chapter 2

BREAKTHROUGH

I knew I wanted to be a writer since I was 13 years old. It was the first time I ever heard (or at least thought I heard) the voice of God speaking to me. He said one word, but it was enough to change my life forever. I was at a youth group service when the youth leader called forward anyone who wanted to hear from the Lord. I thought that sounded pretty cool, plus all my friends were going up, so I bounded up alongside them, wondering whether or not this little magic trick was going to work.

I got on my knees and began to pray. I didn't know quite what to ask God my first time out, and I honestly can't remember the exact words I used at that moment. Most likely it was some awkward utterance of, "God, if You have something to tell me, I'm all ears." I remember sitting there, listening to the music play in the background, while everyone around me continued to pray earnestly. I began to wonder if maybe I was doing it wrong. Maybe I had to pray a longer prayer than that to get the God of the universe to notice me. But then something happened that would begin my life of knowing that God is real, while at the same time wondering if I was just making it all up in my head.

I heard God say something.

It wasn't an audible voice, but more like an explosion of a word in my head. I couldn't think of anything else, I couldn't even notice the music anymore. All I could hear was one word, like a mantra, playing over and over and over again inside my brain, like a jackhammer with no off switch.

"Writer."

That's all I heard, constantly, for probably two minutes. I was shocked, and I wondered why so many people were still praying around me. I thought they should just shut up and listen for a second, because obviously God was in a talking mood at the moment. I turned to my older sister who was kneeling next to me, still in fervent prayer, and I nudged her.

"Danielle!"

She reluctantly opened her eyes and looked at her annoying brother.

"I think I just heard God speak to me. I think He told me I'm going to be a writer!"

Her eyes rolled. "Great, now shut up. I'm praying."

She swung her head back and continued on with her heavenly petition, but this time I didn't even care that she had been a jerk. I had just heard God speak, and that was about the coolest thing ever.

"GOD SPEAK"

I should probably stop for a moment and mention this whole "God spoke to me" business. I am always a bit leery whenever I hear those words, because I have had so many people say that "God gave me this song" or "God gave me this poem," only to then realize that either they are mistaken, or God is a lousy poet or songwriter.

I now understand that God may very well give us ideas, but often our talent (or lack of it) gets in the way of His musings. But while we cringe inwardly, God smiles and delights in the fact that His children took the time to listen to Him, and tried their best with what He gave them. I think we're often more interested in the end result than God is. He seems to care more about faith and obedience than how wonderful or talented we are.

When I talk about God "speaking" to me, it is with great trepidation and not a little doubt. After all, what I'm hearing are really my thoughts, but to me, they are magnified beyond normal thoughts. They dominate my mind, and at first I was very hesitant to chalk them up to God, but the more I acted on them, the more I began to differentiate between what really was just me thinking stuff and what the Almighty was whispering to me. Jesus mentions that His sheep know His voice, and the more I hear it, the more I know it. (See John 10:4.)

But there is certainly a leap of faith that must be made, especially early on, and more than a few times you're going to look like an idiot. Fortunately, my kids make themselves look like idiots all the time, and I never judge them for it. In fact, I love them even more. God does too.

So that one word started me on a long and torturous journey toward a dream that would one day be fulfilled, just not quite as I had expected. All through high school I wrote countless short stories, then moved on to books (very bad ones, mind you) in my college years. I then went to graduate school to learn how to write movies (as well as to avoid the inevitable—I knew that eventually I was going to have to get a real job). I wrote and I wrote and I studied and I read every book about writing I could get my hands on. I was a sponge for storytelling. I loved the nuance of narrative and the power inherent in a well-told story. I loved character development and plot twists and dilemma and action.

THEN ONE DAY...

But then one day in December 2005, something happened to me that had never happened before. I ran out of ideas.

During that time, I would write the ideas that came to my mind in an "idea book," because I was always bursting with new ideas for stories and books and screenplays and didn't want to forget the ideas until the time came when I could use them. I had just finished my latest screenplay when I returned to my idea book to try and figure out what to work on next. By this time I had written five full-length books and about eight or nine screenplays, and I was just starting to get good—in my own humble opinion. But as I looked through my old ideas, I became disheartened, then upset, and finally downright nervous. I had no more good ideas left.

So I tried to come up with some new ones. Nothing. Idea block.

One evening I brought up the issue with my wife, Jenell. Without missing a beat, she asked me a simple question. "Why don't you ask God for an idea?"

It was probably the dumbest piece of advice I had ever received. Ask God for an idea? Why would I do that? He created me with a creative spirit; it was my job to come up with the ideas, execute them, and then give Him all the glory. That's how the game works. The only people who ask God for ideas are people who aren't creative enough to come up with one on their own. And even then, it never works. No, God wasn't interested in giving ideas to people. That was our job to do for Him. The idea of doing this actually made me angry.

Fortunately, I was in a desperate situation. I'm something of a producing junkie; so if I don't have something to work on, I get irritable fast. So that night, as I lay down to go to sleep, I prayed the most non-religious prayer in all of history.

"God, if you've got an idea, I guess I'll take it."

With that I closed my eyes and went to sleep.

Five minutes later I was downstairs at my kitchen table frantically trying to write out the idea that was exploding in my brain. It was born out of all this crazy stuff my parents and wife had been telling me about when they came back from these strange conferences in Toronto, Canada.

My aunt and uncle had recently received gold teeth in a church service (don't worry, I'll deal with that in the next chapter), and my whole world of intellectualized faith was beginning to be challenged. Originally, as it came that night, it was going to be a television show about crazy stuff people believe in all different religions. But over the next few weeks and months, the idea began to morph into a short film about the crazy stuff *Christians* believe.

The only problem with this idea was that it had all the earmarks of something that was decidedly not in my creative wheelhouse. It was a documentary. I like fiction. It was Christian in theme. I like making stuff for the "real world." It was a film. I like writing films, not shooting them; in truth, I had never before even picked up a camera. It required money. I had none. It required contacts. I had none. It was about crazy stuff. I liked normal stuff.

So I did the only thing that seemed reasonable. I ignored the idea entirely. I walked away from it because I didn't want to do it. Deep down I knew I *should* do it and that I *would* do it someday; after all, it was an idea that, well, I *think* God gave me. But it just didn't seem right for me. Not right then anyway. It was a back burner idea. Something I could do once I was a little more established.

Little did I know that in four months, I would have the most insane encounter of my life, and this future idea would become a *now* idea.

THAT CRAZY CHURCH IN TORONTO

I wound up in Toronto because of my wife. She came to me one day and said she would stop asking me to go to conferences with her if I just came to this one that was coming up in May. It was some prophetic thing, and it was at that crazy church in Toronto, so I had absolutely no interest in it whatsoever. Plus, I hate conferences. It's like church for eight hours straight. Who wants to do that? But the thought of never being asked or dragged to one of them again compelled me to go just this once. And maybe I'd hear some crazy stories for that movie I was never going to make.

It should be noted here, in case you may not know, that the church I was going to visit is one that has had its share of controversy. Revival broke out there in 1994 and pretty much continues to this day in some form; it was a revival that ticked off a lot of people. The main problems, as I understood, were the manifestations that came upon people when they were "touched" by God. It didn't happen to everyone, by a long shot, but it certainly happened to a lot of them. While most people just laughed their heads off from the joy they were feeling, others did strange things: shouting, moaning, shaking, and generally making noise. This was a big no-no for religious types, obviously, and it led to a lot of people being upset about what was happening at this crazy church. Many people got "drunk" in the spirit and were so inebriated that they couldn't even drive home. I won't lie to you, it was a weird place for someone like me.

And it was this weird place that I was now trekking to with my family. In a normal universe, I wouldn't have been caught dead in a church like this. Like I said, I liked things simple, stable, and above all, normal. I had heard enough people railing against this "movement" to be wary of it, but there was one undeniable fact that I didn't quite know how to deal with. My family was being radically transformed at this place, and it was a transformation that only God could (or would) do.

My aunt and uncle had received gold teeth, which was the event that began the eventual healing of a horribly broken marriage. My parents and sister and wife were all going and coming back absolutely on fire for the things of God. My dad had a 40-year addiction to pornography obliterated in the twinkling of an eye. Something was changing in all of them, and all of the changes were for the better.

When I turned my critical eye to this church and did my research, I found people like Hank Hanegraaff saying that the devil was behind all this stuff. But then I looked at my family and friends, all of whom were being touched in radical, deep, and very profound ways, and were moving into a deeper, more loving relationship with Jesus Christ, and I had to respectfully disagree with the Bible Answer Man. If the devil was behind this stuff, I don't think a deeper relationship with the living God would be the outcome. I don't think pornography addiction would be annihilated. I don't think marriages would be restored.

I didn't know much of the Bible by heart, but I did know that Jesus once said that a good tree cannot bear bad fruit, just as a bad tree cannot bear good fruit. My family was experiencing very good fruit, so the devil couldn't be behind all of it. That simply wasn't logical.

So it was with a small dose of curiosity and a heavy dose of skepticism that I went to a conference with the "crazy Christians," as I viewed them. And it was exactly as I expected it to be.

I spent most of my time over the next three days being ticked off at what was happening around me. No one would shut up! I wanted to hear the preachers preach, but the people sitting around me kept laughing or making noises. I couldn't concentrate. Then they'd start shaking, twitching, or flailing their arms all over the place, and I knew I had officially entered the nuthouse. I don't care what kind of fruit was coming from this place, these people were insane. And to top it all off, my wife and sister were twitching like maniacs as well! I, of course, couldn't even get a static shock from the carpet. How could

God be behind this craziness? I was certain most of what these people were doing was to either get attention or make themselves look more "spiritual" than the rest of the crazies.

At the end of each night, they would offer ministry to whoever wanted it. At least there was some order to this. We would all line up as members of the prayer team for the church would move among us and pray for us. This being a "prophetic conference," the prayers were of the prophetic persuasion. Needless to say, I was intrigued to see what these people were going to pray over me.

The first shocking thing was that everyone who prayed for me seemed to be 20 years old or younger. The second shocking thing was that they were all really good at praying for me. Every single one of them, without fail, over three nights, had the same thing to say to me. Every prayer was some iteration of, "There's something on a shelf gathering dust, and God wants you to take it down and do what you're supposed to do," or, "You're avoiding the race, but God wants to give you the baton and He wants you to run with it." It was bizarre. And the best part was, all of them ended their prayers with, "And you know what I'm talking about." I certainly did.

This was helpful in nudging me forward a little bit on this short film God had given me an idea for, but it could still all be coincidence. And these people were all crazy, right? Obviously, I had to take that into consideration.

ANGEL BREAKTHROUGH

But then I met Breakthrough.

It was the last night of the conference, and everyone was being particularly Charismatic during worship that night.

I figured the best thing to do was just close my eyes so I wouldn't have to watch it, and since I was in church, I figured I'd try to get something out of the worship. So I stood in the back with my eyes closed, when all of a sudden the worship stopped. One of the speakers, a little, older guy named Bob Jones (who had come through his own share of controversy in the past), had come onstage and grabbed the microphone.

He proceeded to tell all of us that an angel had just entered the building. His name was Breakthrough, and he had been in Nigeria for the past ten years. He had just come over here with a bunch of his angel buddies (I'm not making this up), and they were going to be traveling across North America for the next year looking for hearts that were turned to the things of God. Then he told us all to just keep praising the Lord and let them do whatever it is they want to do. Bob Jones then walked off stage.

This was almost too much to bear. Who did this guy think he was? How did he know an angel had come in? How did he know his name? How did he know where he was from? What he was doing here? And everyone was going crazy because they actually believed him. Did anyone have even a shred of critical thought left in this place? Total insanity. The whole lot.

Worship started back up, and I closed my eyes again. Let's just say I wasn't in the most "receptive" of states at that moment. I was perhaps the most critical person in the entire building, actually.

It was during this state of pious judgment that someone walked in front of me. I could see the light change a bit with my eyes closed, and I instinctively opened my eyes. No one was there. That was weird. So I closed them again, and there, just to my left, was an outline of...someone. I could make out his faint shadow, and he just stood there, about 5 feet away from me, looking in the opposite direction. But he stood stock still, and I stared at him with my eyes closed. I opened them again. Nothing. Closed them. There he was.

Suddenly he turned to me and walked right up to me. Again, all I could see was his outline, like a hazy shadow, but now I could *feel* him. Standing in front of me was easily the most intense individual I had ever encountered. His fists were clenched and he was on fire with intensity—he crackled with it. I half expected him to break through a wall at any moment. Then it hit me, that the guy who was just onstage actually knew what he was talking about. To this skeptical, discerning, practical college professor, there was no longer any doubt about it. Breakthrough was standing right in front of me.

I didn't know what to say, so I didn't say anything. I stood there in awed silence. I kept opening my eyes, saw nothing, then closed them again. He was still there. Every time. Then he spoke to me. It wasn't audible, but was that familiar explosion of words in my head, where everything else is drowned out but the phrase.

"Are…you…ready?"

I had no idea what he was talking about. But I was raised in the church, so I knew enough that if an angel ever asks you a question, you just say yes. I nodded my head.

"Are…you…ready?"

"Yes." Still no idea what it is I'm ready for.

Then I saw his hands reach up, and although I couldn't feel anything, I knew he was grabbing my head. He then screamed in my face, and it was as if every pore in my body cried out along with him.

"ARE YOU READY!"

"Yes," I replied, "But ready for what?" I spoke this out loud.

He stared at me for a moment. A scared young man and a super intense angel. Then he said the words that would forever change my life.

"Make that movie."

And Breakthrough drifted away.

I had never experienced anything like this before, and I realized it was ending, so in my mind I thought, "Wait!" and instantly he was back in front of me. But something had obviously changed. Breakthrough wasn't intense anymore. Instead, he was the most tender, loving individual I had ever met. He oozed tenderness. I could see his hand reaching out to mine, and then I heard a soft whisper in my head that was almost clearer than the shouting had been.

"What do you want, what do you need? I'll stay with you all night if you need me to."

It was at that moment that I realized I had called him back for no good reason other than I didn't want the experience to end, and now I felt like an idiot. So I mumbled something about how I just thought this was really cool, and Breakthrough just stood there, waiting. It was then that I realized that he was probably waiting for me to release him, so I told him OK, he could go now. He then drifted out of my view and to the left.

WHAT HAPPENED?

I didn't know what to do with myself. I remember opening my eyes and turning to my wife and my father, and they immediately realized that something had happened to me. Apparently, I was white as a ghost and a little bit shell-shocked. I told them that I had to go be by myself for a little bit because something crazy just happened to me, and I slipped away upstairs to the balcony area.

There was no one up there—everyone was still downstairs worshiping with great abandon—and I went to the farthest corner and sat down on the floor with my back to the wall. My head was swimming. What had just happened? I knew what had happened was completely, 100 percent real, but I couldn't wrap my mind around it. This kind of thing happens to other people—the crazy people at this conference—not to me. Not to a college professor. Not to someone who has never felt anything in church other than slight annoyance at those around him.

I remember praying the simplest prayer then. It was the prayer of a boy masquerading in a man's body. I simply asked, "God, what are You doing to me?" All pretense had vanished within me, and I only wanted to know what was going on. Immediately a picture erupted in my mind, and I heard a voice that was so real it could have been audible. I saw a young boy and his father in a field playing catch with a baseball. No one knew that this was my favorite memory as a child, playing catch with my dad in the backyard. It was the memory of safety and innocence and the height of my extreme trust that my dad was the greatest person in the world. The voice asked me a very simple question, but as soon as I heard it I burst into tears.

"Do you want to play catch?"

It was as if every ounce of pride I had left was being squeezed out of me by the weight of God's love for me at that moment. I no longer cared if anyone saw me crying, or knew that I had just talked with an angel, or even knew that I was still a boy inside longing to go back to the way things used to be; to a place where playing catch with my dad was the pinnacle of existence because it meant I could just hang out with him.

My whole life I had wanted that kind of relationship with God, but He was always too distant, too invisible, too spiritual, and too stuck in my head to make that desire any kind of reality. But here He was, forcing a picture into my mind of what He really thought of me. I was His kid. He was my Dad. And He wanted to hang out with me.

So we played catch for a while, I don't know how long. But I cried like a baby the whole time, and for the first time I understood what His love for me actually felt like. It was no longer in my head, it was no longer "head love"; it had reached down to my very soul. I was His entirely. Lead on, Master.

After a while I heard Him speak again. This time, there was a gentle purpose, but again, the words filled my head in a way that could only be Him.

"Get up."

I stood up, wiping tears from my face.

"Go to the edge of the balcony."

I walked forward.

"Now look."

I looked down. Below me were nearly 2,000 people who looked like they were completely out of their minds. They were *charismaniacs* in the best and worst way. They twitched, laughed, shouted, and danced around like 4-year-old children.

I looked at that crowd of people, who I had been judging mercilessly just 30 minutes earlier, with new eyes. All I saw was hurt, heartache, pain, fear, doubt, and....

I looked away. This is what the Father saw all the time. He saw past the pretense, past the charades, past the posturing, and into the very heart. Immediately His voice rattled through my brain once again.

"Will you make it for them? Will you make it for My people?"

"Yes," I answered. "I'll do whatever you want me to do."

In truth, I had no idea what He wanted me to do. Sure I knew I couldn't run from this movie anymore, but I didn't know what He had in store for me with it either. I thought I was going to make a short film about weird stuff. Little did I know that He had much bigger plans for it—and me—than I could have ever dreamed.

Chapter 3

GOLD DUST IS EVERYWHERE!

When you finish editing a film, you're not actually finished. The creation of something this massive, into which you have poured nearly two years of your life, leaving your family behind as you travel the world, constantly thinking about how everything fits together, what goes where, how the story will play out...well, let's just say you're not exactly seeing the finished product clearly at that point. You think it's perfect, but the reality is usually a little more bleak.

You need fresh eyes to come in and look at this 90 minutes of film and tell you what they don't get, don't understand, or simply what bored them to tears. You hope all they say is how wonderful it is, but that never happens, because, like I said, it's never perfect the first time out. So you swallow your pride and hope the criticism doesn't hurt too much.

When I first finished *Finger of God,* I had no idea how people would react. There had never really been a movie like this, at least nothing about the subject of miracles that had been put together in this way. So I didn't know if I had a strange, quirky movie or something of real power and potency. My honest thought was that I would be lucky if 1,000 people saw this film in my lifetime.

But I wanted to make sure I was putting out something that worked on some level, so I piled around 30 friends, colleagues, and acquaintances into a classroom at Judson and hit the play button. Ninety minutes later, the lights came up and I received my first ever standing ovation. My sister and brother-in-law came to me, tears in their eyes, and hugged me. Some people were too emotional to even speak to me. One friend of mine was receiving prayer in the corner, and she was wailing loudly. I found out later she was being delivered from a "spirit of religion" (think, fundamentalism).

NEVER THE SAME AGAIN

At that moment, I thought two things:

1. I think this movie might be onto something.

2. Things are never going to be the same again.

Later that night, I started to read the comment sheets I had passed out, and boy, for a group of people who had been so overwhelmed by the film, they sure had a lot of specific opinions about it. One opinion, above all others, though, stood out to me.

Those first 15 minutes are going to be a problem.

Let me pause and explain in case you haven't seen *Finger of God*. I think you'll soon understand why that 15 minutes of video have been a continuous thorn in my side. Basically, the first 15 minutes of *Finger* covers what I initially thought the entire film was supposed to be about. Remember those "weird things Christians believe" I mentioned earlier? Well, this is it. Simply documenting what people were claiming probably wouldn't have been so bad had I not, by the time I was done filming, realized that, well, I think I believe it too. So what are these strange things? In *Finger of God,* there are four in particular:

1. People miraculously get gold teeth.

2. Gold dust appears out of nowhere.

3. Manna shows up out of thin air.

4. Gigantic gemstones (as well as little ones) suddenly appear.

If you've never heard of this before, your first thought is probably similar to mine. That's insane. If you're a true skeptic, your next thought will be how you can disprove these claims. If you're discerning, though, you have to suspend your disbelief for a brief time to truly consider both the circumstances as well as the facts. You must approach these claims with an open mind, but not rush headlong into them simply because I say it's true.

Cautious discernment mixed with a fertile heart and a willingness to acknowledge that God is His own Person and can do whatever He likes, regardless of whether or not we are uncomfortable with it, must be our approach. At least, that's what I tried to do when I started out to film this stuff.

The only insight I can give on these things for certain is my experience with them. When you make a movie like *Finger of God*, you start to hear more stories of the supernatural than the average bear, so for one, the sheer number of occurrences I have heard from normal people who have no ministry at all is fairly overwhelming evidence. But in the end, I can only speak to what I saw and what happened in front of me.

First, the Gold Teeth

This phenomenon of people receiving gold teeth has been happening, as far as I know, since the "outpouring" began in Toronto Airport Community Church (TACF) in 1994 (the same place I met my very intense friend, Breakthrough). Thousands of people have claimed to receive gold teeth, and among those thousands are two who are very close to me— Aunt Patsy and Uncle Bob.

Now the skeptic in me is quite willing to call everyone else claiming this liars or misinformed. Indeed, when I filmed John and Carol Arnott, the senior pastors of TACF during the outpouring, John told me something that I had not heard before. They were as interested as anyone in finding out if this gold teeth experience was actually happening, and they hired an outside service to come and investigate the claims as an impartial jury.

What they found was,

- Roughly one-third of the people had received dental work containing gold in the past, and they simply forgot about it amid the hubbub and excitement of the moment.

- Roughly one-third of the claimants experienced their gold teeth "fading" back to normal teeth for whatever reason.

- But one-third of the claimants had received no dental work, and still had gigantic gold teeth shining in their mouths.

Far from discrediting the occurrences, I found this information to be quite helpful. It meant the people in charge were as curious about the truth as I was. It also cemented what I had previously thought: that not every claim of the miraculous was legitimate. Still, there was one-third of thousands of testimonies that I had to contend with.

But even had every other claim been proved false, I still had to face the fact that my aunt and uncle, my own flesh and blood, people I had known my whole life and were about as normal as you can get (she's a stay-at-home mom, he's a school superintendent), had gone to church and left with gold in their mouths. Aunt Patsy got one, Uncle Bob got two. This is bizzaro-world to the extreme.

I have found that the thing people rage against the most with this stuff is that it seemingly serves no purpose. Even if we discount the idea that God might just want to do something for the fun of it (Is it that absurd to think such things? After all, we do that all the time, and we were created in His image.), we are still left with a few "reasons." Many people I have talked to who have received gold teeth feel that it is a constant reminder that He touched them, that He loves them, and that to Him, they are a treasure—it drives them closer into His arms.

To the outside observer, it seems random, superfluous, and dumb. There are starving children all over the world and you're telling me God is going to put gold in someone's mouth? If He's willing to do that, why won't He drop a few hundred dollars into every beggar's hands? Wouldn't that be more helpful? So many scoff, throw it off as lunacy, or at worst, attribute it to the devil. He's trying to trick people with fake signs and wonders—get their minds off God and onto this superficial stuff.

Good argument; but based on the people I have talked to, based on the experience of my aunt and uncle, it doesn't hold water. While it is true that for some *observers* the action leads to an unhealthy obsession with chasing after signs and wonders, to the *receivers*, it brings a deeper sense of His love for them, and they are humbled, exhilarated, and profoundly affected. I've never met anyone yet who wants to give it back.

ALL IN THE FAMILY

My aunt and uncle went to Toronto in a last ditch effort to save their marriage. Uncle Bob had a tumultuous, abusive upbringing, and as a result became somewhat tumultuous and angry as an adult. Aunt Patsy was commonly referred to as the "super Christian" in our family, and together they obviously had their struggles. Pat struggled with Bob's anger issues, and Bob struggled with a deep sense of shame and guilt that he was, in some ways, a spiritual outcast compared to Pat. His personal issues clouded his sense of self-worth, and that only made things worse. By the time they entered the doors in Toronto, it was do-or-die time. God had to show up for them, or it was over. At this point, only God could save their marriage.

At one point in the service, John Arnott took the stage and announced that he thought God had just released gold teeth in the church, and he told everyone to check their mouths. My aunt and uncle did no such thing. When I talked to them about it afterward, they had very different takes on why they didn't check their own mouths even while those around them did. Aunt Patsy told me that her spiritual life, she was convinced, was based on faith. God wouldn't do something like that to her; *it's not how He worked with her.* She knew He hadn't done something like that, nor did she particularly care for it, because the whole concept of getting gold teeth was so completely not for her.

At least that's what she thought *before.* Later in the service, on a lark, their son had her open her mouth so he could check. My cousin, Bobby, took one look in his mother's mouth and his eyes turned wide with shock. "You got a whopper!" I think that was his exact quote.

No one bothered to check Bob's teeth. As he told me, even after his wife got a gold tooth, it never even occurred to him that God would do something like that to him because, well, God didn't do those kinds of things to people like him. There was no way God could love him *that* much. Strangely enough, as his wife walked by him to go up to the front of the stage to testify what had just happened to her, my uncle recalls smelling an odor similar to what you smell at a dentist's office when they are drilling. It wasn't until later that night as they were leaving the church that someone in their party asked Bob to open his mouth so they could check, just in case.

That's when they discovered that he had gotten *two* gold teeth. Neither Patsy or Bob knew quite how to handle it or what it meant, but they were overjoyed that God would touch them in such a strange, unique way. Shortly after, they received a word my father felt he had gotten during a time of prayer for them. The word was simple, yet powerful. "Pat, I have seen your faithfulness, and I have seen your struggles. I want you to know how proud I am of you, how much I love you, and this gift is, in a sense, your gift for years of loving Me despite what it cost you."

Then it was Bob's turn.

"Bob, I want you to realize something very important. You have always felt left out, in a way. You have believed that Pat has earned My love while you have not, and you feel like she is more highly favored in My eyes than you. But I want you to realize that I gave you *a double portion* of what I gave to her. I did this not because you deserve it, but because I love you so very much."

Instantly, their hearts melted. This event, this strange occurrence that many well-meaning Christians have decried as demonic, was the single event that began the complete restoration of their marriage. They are happily married to this day, and they both have a deeper sense of the Father's love for them, which of course allows them to love each other more effectively. After all, you can't give love to others if you don't know love yourself.

Next up, the Gold Dust

I remember quite clearly one of my first personal encounters with the stuff. I was filming *Finger of God* early on, and I went to a meeting in Chicago to try and capture random "signs and wonders." I didn't go trying to capture gold dust in particular, but was just curious to see what God might decide to do while my camera was rolling. At this point in my film career, I didn't have a lot of faith that God would show up and do something for my camera; I just hoped He would. I had brought two of my students from Judson with me to help. When we arrived, I took off my black coat and put it in the corner on top of one of the student's coats, and the other student put his on top of mine. The coat on top of mine was made of cotton sweatshirt material.

The meeting hadn't started yet, and the worship team was simply practicing. I walked around a bit, set up some cameras, and talked to my guys about what we'd be trying to do that night. At one point, I went back to my coat to get something, and when I lifted the sweatshirt off my coat, I saw that my coat was covered with gold dust. I called the students over and showed them, and none of us knew what to think. As would happen with me more than once, I was so shocked that I completely forgot to film it!

At that meeting, as well as others I attended and filmed, gold dust regularly appeared, usually on random people in the audience. Rarely did it fall on the person speaking. I remember being fascinated by this substance, as well as the apparent randomness of where it would appear. Sometimes I saw people freaking out about a random fleck of something that sort of sparkled like gold, and everyone would crowd around to look at this tiny, microscopic thing, and I remember thinking, "See, this is why people think you all are nuts." It's unfortunately quite true that many people are so hungry for the supernatural, they will grasp at any straw hoping that it's the real thing.

DISCERNMENT AND WISDOM

This mentality is usually what turns people off to these things. There is a common belief that many Charismatics simply "check their brains at the door" when they go to church, and for some people, this is very true. But it is not the call Jesus gave us. He said to love Him with all your heart, soul, and *mind*. We are to react to what is happening around us with discernment and wisdom, but we must also make certain our hearts are positioned as children. That thought, that we must become like children, is fairly misunderstood I think.

Hard-core Charismatics tell you that you need to be willing to believe anything (when in reality what is really happening is that they *simply* believe everything). But when I see how my children interact with the world around them, they don't believe everything they see. In fact, I have shown them things before that have been sent to me from people, things that very well could be supernatural, and they take one look and say something like, "It looks like sand." They see no desperate need to believe in the supernatural to prove they are right about anything, but instead readily believe that if God chooses to do something supernatural, then yeah, of course it can happen.

Another argument I often hear when people watch my film and don't want to believe this stuff is that it appears to be only happening in the United States. Americans are rich compared to much of the world, and therefore it doesn't make sense that God would give us "gold" when the streets of Calcutta are filled with starving homeless men, women, and children. This is proof, they say, that only charlatans are behind this.

This mentality is probably my fault. When I was making *Finger of God*, remember, I had no expectation that anyone would actually *watch* the movie. The idea that millions around the world would see these things I captured and would in turn dissect them in detail was as far from my thinking as the earth is from the moon. I was just trying to tell a compelling story. I wasn't creating an exposé; I wasn't making a film documenting hard evidence.

Gosh, when Heidi Baker asked me what this movie was about just before I started our interview, my lame answer was, "Miracles...I think." I was filming the journey of one man who was slowly coming to grips with the *possibilities* of a limitless God. Once my journey began to leave the realm of the signs and wonders (the film is laid out, basically, in chronological order), I didn't want to return to them, or even search for them.

Of course, I kept hearing of signs and wonders happening everywhere I went—Africa, Eastern Europe, Australia, South America, China—but I was no longer pursuing them as subjects because the miracles I was encountering now were way better and more exciting than shiny objects. But of course the way the film plays out, I can understand why people think that they're only happening in America, because that is all I showed.

When I was filming *Furious Love*, for instance, my crew and I were walking with some friends on the streets of Jakarta, Indonesia. A bunch of beggar children approached us for money, and we couldn't give them any without causing a near riot. But we could pray for them, and that's what we did. We laid our hands on their heads, prayed for God's blessing over them, His protection over them, and His provision for them. When we finished, the kids started freaking out, because suddenly their hands were covered in gold dust.

When I showed *Finger of God* at Judson University (an American Baptist institution), over 20 students had gold dust show up on them afterward. Almost none of them had grown up in Charismatic circles, and no one quite knew what to do when it happened. None of them screamed that it was from the devil or that someone must have come by and sprinkled it on them unknowingly. They just worshiped God even more.

I have had hundreds of people approach me with their own stories, their own experiences that seem straight out of a sci-fi movie. These are all normal, wonderful people. They don't expect me to put them in my next movie; they just want to talk to someone who will probably believe them. In every case, the act brings them closer to the Father's heart and love for them.

Third, Manna

Gold dust and gold teeth were, by the time I was putting my movie together, fairly common occurrences for me and my camera. I had heard and seen enough of it with my own eyes to be confident that much of it wasn't coming out of deceptive practices. But manna was a whole new ballgame when I encountered it.

Manna proves tricky for the true skeptic because, well, it *is* in the Bible. The only plausible defense against it can be if you don't believe God is in the business of miracles anymore, which, I'm afraid, is becoming less and less plausible if you sit down and really look at the facts. Most Christians, for instance, even secessionists, would agree that the incredible growth of Christianity in China is a good thing. The fact that signs and wonders and miracles are playing an enormous role in the growth could prove problematic for the true blue disbeliever in the miraculous. But I digress….

For me, supernaturally receiving manna from God was tricky, because as far as I could tell, only one couple, Harold and Kaye Beyer, had this experience. They were an older couple from Idaho who had been seeing manna instantly appear either in Harold's hands or in his Bible for over 36 years. They kept it secret for a long time, because they didn't want people to think they were con artists or completely insane. When the truth got out, their world turned upside down. They were a "normal" Lutheran couple who suddenly found themselves kicked out of their church, ostracized from their friends, and considered "dangerous."

When they came to a church in Chicago to speak, I showed up with my camera hoping to capture the manna appearing out of thin air on camera. Hey, a guy can dream, right? By the time the service started, the manna had already appeared. I was bummed, but then I found out that it had happened just outside the meeting in the hallway. About a dozen people were with the couple as they walked, some of whom were friends of mine, when suddenly Harold stopped walking, and everyone gathered around to pray. Not one person had their eyes closed; all were looking at Harold, a nice, unassuming 86-year-old man. He put his hands out in front of him, then suddenly everyone felt a shift in the atmosphere around them, and instantly his hands were overflowing with manna. That night in the service we had communion, and God had provided the bread. This service is featured in *Finger of God*.

So I didn't film the manna appearing, but I had more than ten people verify to me that, yes, they had seen it appear with their own eyes. Everyone's story was the same. Either my friends had all conspired to pull the wool over my eyes (what gain they would get is beyond me), or this supernatural event had actually happened.

Later in the year, I filmed Canon Andrew White, Vicar of Saint George's Church in Baghdad (the only Anglican church in Iraq at the time) and a special envoy to the Middle East by the Archbishop of Canterbury. He spoke to me, quite unassumingly, about the time he found out that manna had appeared in the hands of some people he worked closely with at the Pentagon. This was the second occurrence I had encountered, which ultimately led to me including the manna in the finished film.

Finally, the Gemstones

I'm going to be honest with you, the gemstone miracles kind of freak me out. They are so out there, so ridiculously strange, that even now I have a hard time believing in them as real occurrences. But as with nearly everything I have encountered, I have been so inundated with random, normal people telling me their stories, showing me their gemstones, that I have to believe at least some of them are telling the truth. I've looked into their eyes and I've seen the innocence, the awe-struck wonder they have, months or years later, in recalling that moment when their gemstone just "appeared out of thin air" in front of them.

The gemstones I included in *Finger of God* are ridiculously large—50 karats some of them. I have been told that some of them have been taken to jewelers and gemologists for verification, coming back with the verdict that they don't know exactly what they are. They don't contain the minerals that normal, earthly gemstones have. They don't contain the microscopic bubbles of manmade material. Their weight doesn't line up with cubic zirconium. The experts are baffled by what exactly these things are. Again, these are things I *have been told*, so to a large degree I must take people's word for it. Because I want to get to the bottom of this issue myself, I plan to conduct follow-up research on these claims for a new series.

I have read reports of people purporting to have gems falling in their meetings and were later caught planting gems throughout the sanctuary. Herein lies the difficulty for so many people. We know there are crooks out there, we know that many people want to believe in the supernatural so badly that they will suspend their own disbelief to accept something as real despite their better judgment. People lie. This is a fact that we cannot get around.

But then again, I have talked to so many normal, everyday people who have seen with their own eyes, gems materializing in the air then dropping in front of them. Others have gone to the kitchen for a coffee refill and when they return to their home office found a gemstone sitting next to their keyboard. Some have felt a gem hit their foot as they sat listening to someone speak in church. These people have no reason to lie, and many have a hard time even admitting what happened because they know how unbelievable it is. Those are the people I listen to. Those are the ones I find convincing. And the sheer number of them (I've personally encountered hundreds at this point), outweighs my own natural, fleshly objections.

THE FIRST 15

As I stared at the comment sheets in front of me, my heart sank. Everyone was warning me about those first 15 minutes, warning me that this was going to be a problem for a lot of people. Their advice: take it out. The rest of the movie was so fantastic, they said, it didn't need the added weight, and I didn't need the added stress of these oddities. Too many people, they warned, would turn the movie off after those first 15 minutes because they would be so skeptical, so offended by this stuff, that they wouldn't give the rest of the movie a chance.

I knew they were right, and I resolved to take out that section. But as I was editing the film, I had a conversation with my father that altered the film, and in a way, my entire life. I told him about my decision to jettison those troublesome first 15 minutes, and he asked me this fateful question: "Son, tell me, do you believe that the things in those first 15 minutes are from God?"

"Yeah, I think I do."

"Then you have to include them. It's not up to you to decide what people can or cannot believe. You simply have to show them what you experienced and let them decide. Let the Holy Spirit work through them, give them ears to hear. If they reject it, so be it. At least you can say you were obedient."

That was it. I knew I had to do it. I also knew I was setting myself up for a major headache. Boy was I right about that.

For some reason, I seem to have become the patron saint of all things wacky supernatural. I get it to a point. I mean, no one else made a movie about this stuff, so why wouldn't I be the object of the firestorm? But at the same time, I struggle with these things just as much as the next guy. I was skeptical about all of the things I was hearing when I started making these films, and to some degree I still am. I have seen people lie. I have seen people stretch the truth. I have seen the naked ambition of some evangelists and pastors that I encounter. Trust me, if there is anyone who understands the ugly underbelly of Charismatics and belief in the supernatural, it's me. I've seen all the problems, all the hype, all the manipulation. Why, then, do I still hold fast that God is in the business of doing these strange things today, just as He did strange things in the Bible? Because the ugly isn't all I see.

SUPERNATURAL LOVE AND DANGER

For every manipulative evangelist who is pushing people down on stage and making unsubstantiated claims of the miraculous on television, there are a hundred humble, loving pastors and individuals around the world quietly doing God's work, loving the unloved around them, and relying on God to show His love to others, often in miraculous ways. They are not asking for God to give people gold teeth or drop gemstones in their churches, but when it happens, they do what they are supposed to do: praise God, thank Him, and move on to loving the lost.

The real danger of the supernatural is that it can overshadow the natural. We can become so caught up in seeing these things or defending these things that we wind up debating with each other when we should be loving each other. If you want to call me a heretic, I'll take it, as long as you love the person in front of you. I'd love it if you loved me as well, even if you disagree with me, but I understand that your belief system demands that I know that what I believe is false. I get it. But I think you're wrong too. So we are left at an impasse. Either one of us gives, or...or what? We either continue railing against each other, or we wise up and realize that there is a dying world all around us; and in the end, whether or not Aunt Patsy and Uncle Bob really got gold teeth doesn't need to keep us from that dying world.

Look at it this way. I may disagree with my wife about how we should handle our finances. It's a real disagreement, and it has real consequences. But our disagreement should not, cannot, lead us to division and hatred. The Bible doesn't say you're allowed to divorce over financial disagreements. To save your marriage, you're going to need to find a compromise; and above all, you need to stay respectful and loving. The Church is a family, but we're squabbling like children while the world looks on, hoping we'll look outward for a change.

I have never bought the argument made by some Charismatics that if you question these things you are showing a lack of faith. That argument is weak at best, and a total cop out at worst. In First Thessalonians 5:21, Paul tells us to test all things, and hold firm to that which is good. I may test something and find it good. You may test it and find it bad. In the end, we are commanded to "hold fast" to what is good; and what we all agree, and all know to be true, is that what is most good, what is most perfect, is the love found in Jesus Christ. To that we must hold firm no matter what.

LOOK AT THE FRUIT

In the end, I have a very simple formula for figuring out whether I am going to include something in my films or not.

I look at the fruit. Jesus said no good tree can bear bad fruit, just as no bad tree can bear good fruit (see Matt. 7:17). If the root of the miracle is bad, then it is going to lead to heartache, pain, and death. Division, I think, cannot be considered bad fruit, because Jesus' life and miracles caused so much division He was killed for it. But if the root of the miracle is God, then it will lead to faith, love, and hope. It will lead to restoration, not destruction. It will lead to forgiveness, not bitterness. If you don't want to believe that Aunt Patsy and Uncle Bob received a touch from God that day that led to the restoration of their marriage, that is your choice. But don't try to steal their joy away because what happened to them doesn't fit neatly into your own personal experience.

I find it humorous that the very people who often write to me and try to get me to see the error of my ways are the same people who teach their children Bible stories where donkeys talk, iron axe heads float, water pours from rocks, seas part, people are raised from the dead, manna appears out of nowhere for 40 years, shadows heal people, men teleport, a woman turns into salt, wooden rods turn into snakes, bushes burn but aren't consumed, the sun stays in one spot for 12 hours, three men stand in a furnace and live, water is turned into wine, food multiplies…the list goes on. Compared to that stuff, a little gold dust appearing in a place where the presence of God shows up doesn't seem so outlandish after all.

Chapter 4

IT ALWAYS HAPPENS
TO SOMEONE ELSE

Coming out of a background where nothing supernatural, weird, or abnormal really happened to me, I never expected anything like that to start happening to me when I started making movies about the supernatural. That was probably a gross miscalculation on my part, but I honestly thought that I'd simply be filming things that were happening to other people, not me. Again, I had no master plan when I started *Finger of God*, no grandiose ideas to found a production company designed to push the boundaries of Christian media; I was just trying to be obedient to what I felt the Lord told me to do. "Make that movie," He told me, and even though I didn't know what that movie was about exactly, I kept moving forward, trusting that He would eventually show me what to do with it.

Perhaps the thing I love the most about my job is the opportunity to meet some of the most wonderful, inspiring people on the planet. On the other hand, I remember being continually disappointed as a Christian growing up. When I got to know the people I looked up to a little better, they didn't seem as wonderful up close as they did from a distance. Even now, I meet people who may have a thriving, surging ministry, but underneath it all I can sense something amiss. It could be ambition at all costs, greed, pride, or a sense of entitlement. I may not see it on the surface, but I can sense it, and so can my crew.

But occasionally I meet people who blow me away with their humble attitude, their passion for the Lord, and their zeal for holiness and purity. Jason Westerfield is one of those people. I first met him when a mutual friend of ours called me and told me I needed to go to New Haven, Connecticut, where Jason lives, to film with him. I had no idea who Jason was or why I should go film him; but this friend had an amazing track record, and if she said go film him, I would buy my plane ticket, no questions asked.

JASON'S MINISTRY OF MIRACLES

I flew to New Haven and met Jason. He was a nice guy with a beautiful young family, and we spent most of that first day getting to know one another. He told me about how he had become a Christian at age 23, and how the Lord had told him to give up his entertainment career to pursue Him. Jason didn't grow up in a church, so when he became a Christian, he did the only thing that seemed reasonable to him. He read the Bible and prayed. He read stories about men and women who commonly communed and talked with God, who heard His voice and obeyed—Jason figured that was what normal Christians do. He set out to learn how to hear God's voice and develop a personal, intimate relationship with Him.

He told me a story about his first day of "training," as he put it. He went to Huntington Beach early one morning and found a stretch where no one was around. He didn't want to look too strange. He stood in the middle of the beach and prayed for God to speak to him. After a few minutes, he felt like he heard a small voice inside of him tell him to close his eyes. He did. Then the voice said, "Now walk." He did. He walked and walked and walked, all the time with his eyes closed. He knew he was on a deserted beach with no real fear of running into anyone or anything, so he just kept walking slowly forward, eyes closed, waiting for his next instruction.

Suddenly, he felt like he heard the voice say, "Stop." He stopped. He stood still, waiting. Nothing. A minute or so went by, but the voice no longer spoke, and he was starting to wonder if it was just his thoughts, although the Presence of God was on him. He decided to walk again although he hadn't heard anything. He took a step forward and hit a pole with nothing else around. He opened his eyes and realized that he had been hearing the Holy Spirit's voice after all.

Jason practiced walking in God's presence, hearing His voice, and being led by the Holy Spirit in his day-to-day life. In the beginning, the Lord would speak simple things to Jason such as, "Pick up this piece of trash," "Go help this person," "Give this person money and buy them some food," "Take care of your belongings, be a good steward," "Share Jesus with this person and ask if you can pray for him." Jason learned how to abide in God's presence and walk in a friendship relationship with Jesus wherever he was.

COMPLETELY SOLD OUT

That was pretty much how Jason lived for a while, completely sold out to hearing the voice of the Lord, learning to do what God wanted him to do, and trying to obey without question. The Lord told him to live in his car, so he gave away many of his belongings and lived in his car, a homeless person, for months. The Lord told him to get a job at McDonald's, so he did. He was a sharp guy, so they put him on point taking orders. While Jason would be taking orders at the counter, God would speak to him information about people's lives who were ordering their food. He gave over 100 prophetic words and saw three miracles from over the counter—many people gave their hearts to Jesus at McDonald's.

As Jason watched a person mopping, he thought, "At least I don't have to do that." The next day the management asked him to mop. He did. The next week, he watched as someone took out the trash, and he thought, "At least I don't have to do that." The next day his manager asked him to take out all the trash. He did, albeit reluctantly. As he hauled out the garbage, he went by a big pile of dishes that the person doing the dishes couldn't even see over. He thought, "At least I don't have to do that." The next day the manager asked Jason to wash the dishes. With each task more menial than the last, the Lord never stopped taking him lower. He wanted to see how far Jason would go in serving, humility, and obedience with a thankful heart to His voice. Jason was determined to see it through, no matter where God took him or what the cost.

Jason worked at a church for two and a half years as a custodian and then took a job at Red Lobster, where he was a server. For three years he served tables, always looking for opportunities to pray for people. If he overheard a conversation about a health issue, he asked if he could pray for them. He told me many stories of miraculous healings and creative miracles that happened while he prayed for someone with one hand and held a teetering set of dishes in the other. People would come to Red Lobster and ask the management to meet Jason and his wife Jessica (who also worked as a server) to receive prayer. During this time, Jason realized people aren't looking for a religious organization, but for people who know God personally and have power in their lives to help them.

Jason believed that God wanted to "break him" of all earthly desires. All pride and vanity had to vanish in Jason's heart before God could trust him enough with the call He had placed on his life. Jason stayed obedient to God's voice, and by the time I met him in May 2007, the Lord had released him to begin a ministry, which he began full time three months prior.

The next morning, while I sat with his wife, Jessica, and their toddler son eating waffles, Jason sat on a couch in his living room seemingly asleep. I thought how strange it was for someone to sleep on their couch while they had a guest over during breakfast, but I meet a lot of unusual people, so I thought nothing of it. After about 30 minutes, Jason came in and joined us. I asked him if he'd gotten a good nap, and he looked at me a little strangely, then said, "I was praying." This wasn't the first or the last time that I felt like a spiritual moron when talking to Jason.

PRAYER TIME

While he layered syrup on his waffles, Jason explained that during his prayer time, the Lord had shown him where we should go that day. He said God told him He had given us four square blocks in the city, and if we went there today, God would show up. I had no idea where he'd be taking me, so I just said OK, downed my orange juice, and went to get my equipment ready.

About an hour later, I was walking through an enormous courtyard on Yale University's campus. We were in the heart of the city, in the heart of higher learning in America. As we walked, Jason tried to teach me a little about how he does what he does. We saw people standing in groups here and there. We had no plan of action. I carried my camera and a tripod, Jason was mic'd up, and I had no idea what to expect. I hadn't heard of this guy, hadn't seen him pray for people. I was just here hoping that God would do something that I could capture on film.

Jason pointed out the little pockets of people. He said he could go up to that particular group easily, it wouldn't be a big deal. But he only wanted to do what he felt God wanted him to do; so as we walked, he prayed. After a while, he felt God telling him to go to a group of workers who were obviously on their lunch break. There were two of us and about ten workers. I was very glad I had a camera to hide behind.

As we walked up to them, Jason explained to me what was going on inside him. He was nervous, which was a good sign. If he wasn't nervous, he knew it probably wasn't the Lord. God always requires faith on our part, and doing something that seems natural and easy doesn't require a lot of faith. *Step out of your comfort zone, and now you're walking in God country.*

We were 20 yards away from the group and he told me he had no idea what he was going to say to any of them. He'd just have to start talking and hope God would give him something. I thought he was crazy, but we barreled ahead, and I found myself fading behind Jason. This was going to be a disaster, I knew it. I wondered if he knew it too, because he asked me not to film this.

He started talking to them, and they at first looked at us like we were completely bonkers. But as he told them about me and about what I was doing with this movie, suddenly he turned to a woman nearby and began to tell her information he couldn't have known about her life—deep, inner dreams and hopes that weren't vague or cliché. The woman began tearing up. Jason talked about her son, and then the tears really flowed. This was incredible, I thought. How was he doing this? Everyone else sat where they were, watching this event unfold. They obviously knew this woman, and the hard faces that met us were now incredulous, and more than a little shocked. Smiles peeked out here and there as they began to realize that maybe this guy wasn't crazy after all.

HEALING HEARTS AND BODIES

When Jason finished, a couple of other people volunteered themselves for Jason to pray for, and so it went. Several of the people in the group received miraculous healings with nobody touching them and gave their hearts to Jesus. It always happens like this, no matter who I'm filming with. Everyone is hesitant and nervous at first to receive prayer or ministry, but when they see that God isn't going to "zap" them or expose their deepest darkest secrets to the world, but is instead going to lavish them with His love, they can't wait to get prayer.

By the end of this particular little "lesson," we had made ten new friends, and there were smiles all around. We walked away, and Jason simply said, "That was cool." I asked him when he knew what to say, and he told me at first he was just stalling, but then God highlighted the woman, and he knew he was supposed to start with her. He still didn't know what to say, but he turned to her in faith and started talking. As soon as he started, the things about her life gradually unfolded to him by the Holy Spirit.

Around this time, another person whom Jason had met a few days earlier joined us. He was interested in the things Jason was doing, and he decided to tag along. Hey, as long as Jason was cool with it, I was fine. This would just give me another person to hide behind in those awkward moments that were sure to come. We stopped at the steps leading into a dorm in the courtyard and began to talk to each other. Jason and I were in the middle of a conversation when suddenly Jason stood up, went to the top of the steps, and started prophesying. Loudly. I grabbed my camera, got as far away as I could, and watched the events unfold.

People came over and listened for a bit, then some drifted off. Others stayed. A crowd began to form. At first I thought they were really listening, then I realized most of them were students who wanted to get to their dorm but felt bad because it appeared that someone was filming a movie and they didn't want to mess it up. I was told that the previous weekend, the latest *Indiana Jones* movie was being filmed, and there were camera crews and trucks here and there throughout the campus. Maybe they thought this was part of that. Or maybe they just thought we were filming some kind of spoof on religion. Hey, at least they treated us with respect.

For 45 minutes—no joke—Jason prophesied on those steps, his new friend standing next to him silently praying. Then Jason asked if anyone needed prayer for any healing. There weren't any takers. The students surged past him, and he and his friend, realizing no one was coming forward, fell on their faces in prayer and worship. I didn't know what to do, so I just stood there, filmed a little, then walked around admiring the beautiful courtyard on this sunny day. I chuckled as some Japanese tourists gathered around Jason, snapping pictures of him. They saw the camera, saw this guy lying prostrate on the ground, and I can't imagine what they thought was happening. But hey, this is America. Click. We heard this place was different. Click.

THE START OF SOMETHING BIG

After about half an hour, Jason and his friend stood up. I approached them gingerly, wondering what had just happened. Jason started telling me what he saw when he opened his eyes—a gigantic combat boot right next to his head. Like, physically it was right there. His first thought was, what the heck is that? Then suddenly a second combat boot slammed down next to his head. *Uh oh,* he thought.

He looked up and saw the biggest angel he had ever seen in his life. He didn't know they came this big. It was so tall that he had to look up hundreds of feet to see the angel's head. He heard the angel's thundering voice. It rumbled, "We've been waiting for this for a very long time." Jason thought that was pretty cool, and he knew that it was a sign of revival and reformation. This was apparently the start of something big, and here we were at the starting line: a guy three months into full-time ministry and another guy with a camera who had no idea what he was doing. I've said it once and I'll say it again, God's got an awesome sense of humor.

Jason told us about what he saw in the spiritual realm, and boy was it different from what was familiar to me. When he started into it, the other guy got real excited and exclaimed, "I saw that too!" So these two talked to each other and exchanged notes—they both had the exact same vision! And the stuff they saw was so wild; I realized this couldn't be a coincidence. Swords flying through the air, a giant earthquake opening up right through the campus, arrows flying in specific directions—all sorts of craziness.

I just stood there having a hard time believing what I was hearing. I knew this feeling well. Someone gets up in front of the church or at a conference and tells some nutty story about some nutty experience they had, and it blows everyone's minds, including mine. But then I walk away knowing more certainly than ever that stuff like that will *never* happen to me. I don't feel a thing in church. I've never shook, never laughed, never "whoo'd" or "haw'd"; shoot, I've never even spoken in tongues. For me, it's all normal, all the time. Those kinds of experiences are for other people. People who are more "open" to the Spirit. People who are less in control of themselves than I am.

ARE YOU SERIOUS?

After they had commiserated, Jason turned to me. I saw a vague smile come across his face, almost mischievous. He then said the one thing I was least expecting.

"Hey Darren, do you want to see into the supernatural realm?"

"Are you serious?"

"Yeah. I'll pray for you right now and you'll see."

This was it, I thought. *This was the moment of truth.* If Jason prayed for me and I didn't see anything, which would most definitely happen, it would mean one of two things: 1) Either Jason was an especially good con man, or 2) I was going to need to have even more faith that what I was seeing while making this film was real. So it was with a slight sense of trepidation that I replied, "Hit me with your best shot."

He had me take off my glasses. Then he put his hands on my eyes. I was expecting a grand prayer of petition, but all I got was, "Lord, open his eyes and let him see." He kept his hands on my eyes for a second, then said, "Now Darren, just so you know, when you open your eyes, you're going to see into the spirit realm. So don't freak out."

Yeah right, I thought.

He then took his hands off my eyes, and I looked around.

Nothing. Just like I figured.

Then Jason nudged me. He told me to look up near the roof, just between two chimneys.

I did. At first, what I saw didn't quite compute. I remember putting my glasses back on, and it was still there. I took them off, still there. Put them back on…*what was that?*

Here's what I saw. About 10 feet above the roof of a building, I saw what appeared to be little sparks, almost like firecrackers with no sound, popping in the air. Then, instantly, they began to spread like a band to my left. They spread across the sky like a beam of light, and the popping sparkly things now looked like a thick band of tiny fireworks stretching across the rooftop.

"Oh, check out the alley," Jason said excitedly.

I looked into the little alleyway leading out of the courtyard, and there, in the shadows, were more sparkly popping things. I just stood there, dumbfounded. Was this really happening? To me? This stuff happens to other people, not me. I finally asked, "What is that?"

Jason seemed to know. "It's the glory realm." I wasn't sure what that meant, but it sounded good. Then he got real excited.

"Dude, check out behind you!"

I turned around. Just five minutes ago, I had been waiting for Jason and his friend to get up off the ground, and in my boredom, I had walked around a little bit, taking in the beauty of this wide open space in the heart of Yale's campus. It was a sunny May afternoon. But now I could hardly believe what I was seeing. Fully half of the courtyard was covered in a mist, like a fog. The other half was just as it looked five minutes ago.

"What…is…that?"

"That," Jason explained, "is the glory cloud." I had heard of this one. It's the same cloud that appeared every day for the Israelites during their exodus from Egypt, when they had been led through the wilderness by a cloud at day and a pillar of fire at night. Here it was. Right in front of me. I was in such a state of shock, I picked up my camera and we started walking. Not once did it occur to me to turn on my camera and see if I could film this stuff.

I cannot stress how awe inspiring, how entirely disconcerting it is to see a realm of reality that exists just beneath the surface of the natural. Now, of course, I am in utter disbelief that I didn't hit record, but at the time, it was honestly the furthest thing from my mind. I now have a better understanding of those stories in the Bible when God confuses people so they're not quite thinking straight, like the prison guards who simply watched as Peter was led out of prison by the angel in Acts (see Acts 12:9). My mind was a scrambled egg. I knew what I was seeing was real, but that's about all I could understand or comprehend.

GOD'S HERE

When we exited the courtyard, we walked to a traffic light and waited to cross. Jason told me to look to my right. I did. The cloud was there. The entire street was filled with fog. It was following us. Then Jason said something that upon reflection sounds funny, but at the time felt like the most normal idea in the world.

"Well, God's here, so we can pretty much do whatever we want. You're making a movie, right? Why don't we try to find someone in a wheelchair or on crutches?"

"Yeah. Sounds good."

We started walking, this time on the lookout for someone in a wheelchair or on crutches. We soon entered an open, grassy area of the city, and I looked around in vain. What the heck was I supposed to look for? I didn't see anyone in a wheelchair. I trusted that Jason would know who to talk to, but we walked in silence for nearly ten minutes. Nothing.

Jason turned to me, and as he started to speak, my heart fell. Maybe this wasn't going to be a great day after all.

"I don't know about you, Darren, but I'm not getting anything."

That's when we heard the voice behind us.

"Excuse me?"

We turned around and saw a woman approaching us. She asked us for some money for bus fare. That is where the scene begins in *Finger of God*....

Also in the film, just after Jason prays for the bus fare lady, he turns and says, "There's my man. Come on dawg!" He finally saw someone on crutches.

A year-and-a-half later, when I was again filming with Jason in Salem, Massachusetts, for *Furious Love*, I asked him about that day. I wanted to know what led him to pray for me to see into the spiritual realm. Was he acting on faith, like he had with those people earlier in the day? I had told this story in public in the past, and he would occasionally encounter someone who had heard my story who then wanted him to pray for them to see, as if it were some kind of magic trick.

"Jason, what made you do that? Did you just believe God would do it or what?"

There it was—the look I knew well telling me I had just asked one of my more ridiculous questions.

"God told me to."

Ah yes. Of course.

I had always considered myself beyond the scope of having supernatural events happen to me. I was always too analytical, too skeptical to allow something like this to happen to someone like me. But when God decides something, even our own skepticism and hard hearts cannot stop Him. These types of events are not the norm for me by a long shot, but as I position myself in places where God is moving in profound and powerful ways, I no longer believe that encounters like this are not meant for me.

God loves to reveal Himself to us, but it has to be on *His* terms. I am always encountering people who want these experiences to happen to them because, well, they just do. They don't necessarily need them, but they want a powerful experience. They want a story to tell. Or they want, like, a ride. Yet in my experience, these things only happen to people for a purpose. For me, it was another rung in my ladder to belief in the supernatural. I suppose God realized He would be giving me a platform to tell these experiences to the world, and that's why He did what He did. While I have always gone after supernatural occurrences for my films, I rarely despair for an experience myself. I have seen it happen over and over again, where people long after the experiences so much that they cease to long after the Giver of the experiences.

But in the end, the Giver is far more wonderful and far more amazing than the gift. It seems that once we give up on our desperate desire for a supernatural experience and just go after the Lover of our souls, well, that's when He shows up and opens our eyes to the very thing we've laid at His feet.

I think my father put it best when he told me that everyone wants to have those mountaintop experiences, and many people want to live on that mountaintop, but this isn't what God wants for us. At least, He certainly doesn't want us to live there. Nothing grows on a mountaintop; growth only happens the lower you go, and the best growth occurs in the valleys.

I think the same is true for our spiritual lives. Mountaintop experiences, where we have radical encounters with a supernatural God, are some of the most wonderful, needed things for the Body of Christ. Mountain climbers work hard and need an almost obsessive desire to get to the top of the most extreme mountain, but they all realize that once they reach the summit, they cannot stay there or they will die. We must have these experiences with God, but we cannot live indefinitely in these experiences. We must go back down the mountain and join the rest of the world in the valleys and the jungles or forests. That is where our growth will come, that is where we will be nourished, and it is ultimately where we will find each other, which is really what God has been calling us to all along.

Chapter 5

BEING WRONG IS NOT THE
WORST THAT CAN HAPPEN

"Come on, Wilson, you gotta try one thing at least!"

Will Hart was admonishing me, and as usual, I was laughing. I don't think I laugh more with anyone in the world than I do with Will Hart, an evangelist who has accompanied me on various filming trips around the world, and who has become a trusted friend. He is, without question, one of the funniest people I know. He also has a heart that absolutely burns for God and for saving the lost. But today, he was having some fun at my expense.

We were at an enormous outdoor market in Bangkok, Thailand, taking a day off from filming to see some sights. At this particular moment, we were standing in front of a vendor who was offering such delectable delights as fried baby sparrows (with legs and head included), wasps, water beetles, and crickets. The other guys had all tried something, which, of course, meant that my manhood was on the line. I gingerly chose the wasp—since it was the smallest—and crunched down. It tasted like…a wasp. Will bellowed with laughter at my face, and popped another baby sparrow into his mouth. He said it was pretty good, but crushing the skull and dealing with the rubbery feet was kind of nasty.

I had just spent a week with my crew and Will in Bangkok and Pattaya, as we filmed with various ministries who are light in darkness in the truest sense of the word. We spent time with ministries like Nightlight Design, which works tirelessly to get women out of the sex trade and into jobs making jewelry. The goal is to give these women jobs outside of prostitution and to return their dignity.

Whenever I go somewhere to film, there is almost always at least one ministry I visit that is already working in the area. Only occasionally do I go into a place blind, and that is becoming increasingly rare. But even though we may be working with an established ministry in the area, my crew and I almost always hit the streets ourselves. So I go to an area knowing a little about what I am going to capture, but I always want to allow God to do whatever He wants with us—to allow for those "God moments" for which my films are known.

Will Hart was the guy I brought along to help with these God moments. He had lived in Mozambique with Heidi and Rolland Baker and has seen thousands of miracles in his 28 years. He's done a lot of street ministry and evangelism, and he has a giant heart for Thailand, so I figured he would be perfect for this trip. Plus, I knew we were going into a heavy atmosphere, and the more jokesters we could have along with us, the easier it would be for everyone.

We filmed a lot with Will that week—in bars, clubs, and brothels; he wasn't afraid of anything or anyone, and intimidation didn't seem to be in his vocabulary. He has the uncanny ability to instantly make a stranger feel comfortable and unthreatened when he approaches them. I watched in amazement as he approached people—prostitutes and predators—with tenderness and confidence and told them that God wanted to show them how much He loved them. Will is also very prophetic, and he never shied away from speaking prophetic words over people. Many were amazed and left in tears when they heard the words God had for them. It was beautiful to watch all week.

A THING FOR BIRTHDAYS

But there was another occurrence that happened with alarming regularity that caused all of us no small sense of embarrassment and awkward moments. For some reason, this week Will had a thing for birthdays.

I kid you not, with nearly everybody Will encountered, the first thing he tried to do was guess their birthday. Now this wasn't a normal thing for him to do; in fact, he'd never done it before in his life. But for some reason, this week, whenever he met someone, he would get a very strong impression of a particular date, and he was almost certain it was a birth date. So he would approach someone, start a little small talk, and then ask them if, by chance, their birthday was, say, October 3. Every person, without fail, gave him a blank stare, then stated that no, in fact, their birthday was on, like, April 30.

No matter what date he gave, their real birth date was about as far from it as possible.

The first few times it happened was kind of funny. Will would look sheepish but then would barrel forward. I'd usually laugh nervously, inwardly hoping he'd stop doing this stupid birthday thing. But with each new person we met, there came another stab at the birthday. By the end of the week, Will was...I was shocked to see it...frustrated. God was doing great things, but Will couldn't figure out what was going on with the birthdays. He was *certain* that what he was hearing was from the Lord; he knows that voice, he would tell me over and over again. And he had never been this wrong this often in his entire life. What was going on?

We both got the answer on the same day toward the end of our stay in Thailand. That morning, I had a strong sense of what God might be doing, and later in the afternoon Will approached me with the exact same thought. God was teaching us, and me in particular, a lesson.

Without question, the most frequently voiced comment I hear from people when they see my films is some iteration of "Boy, I sure wish stuff like that would happen to me." When I ask them if they ever pray for people around them, the same look of shock and horror that I know so well flickers across their faces. "Oh, I could never do that. It would be terrifying!"

In my experience, though, the people who do these kinds of things on a regular basis—who see someone in need no matter where they are, and approach them to pray for them— are always nervous about what they're about to do. It's never easy to pray for someone, especially if you don't know them. But often, even when we do know them, even if it is a member of our own family, we become so paralyzed by fear that we are grounded by inaction.

Jesus was quite clear that we would "do greater things" than He did. (See John 14:12.) This seems like a clear directive to walk confidently into the dark unknown and face our own unbelief head on. Having talked with countless Christians over the years, I am now convinced that the overwhelming reason more Christians are not stepping out in their faith, not praying for full blown healing and intervention in someone's life, and generally do not act on Jesus' admonition to do greater things than He did, is because we are terrified, utterly horrified by the prospect of being wrong, looking foolish, and in no small way, making God look weak. We either fear man, or we fear a silent God. Either way, it is fear that is keeping us from a life of faith.

ROGER

I remember a story Kevin Dedmon, a staff member at Bethel Church in Redding, California, told me when I was filming *Finger of God*. He was standing on the sidewalk in town one day, waiting for the rest of his ministry team to show up, when he saw a man coming toward him on the sidewalk. He heard what he felt was quite clearly the voice of the Lord repeating the same word over and over again.

"Roger."

"Lord, is that you? Is this a word of knowledge?" he asked.

"Roger, Roger, Roger," was all the voice repeated, over and over again.

Kevin wrestled with God as the man approached; after all, he had never done anything like this before. He had never had a word of knowledge before, but he knew he had a choice at this moment. Step out in faith, or back away to protect his dignity. He took a deep breath and stopped the man.

Or at least, he tried to.

"Excuse me, is your name Roger?"

The man looked at him like he was a nut or some kind of predator. He kept walking, and Kevin had to turn to keep up with him. The guy wanted nothing to do with Kevin and even crossed the street to get away from him. Kevin was left standing there, dejected and embarrassed, and mumbled this prayer, "Thanks God. Thanks a lot for that one. Now I look like a total idiot."

Almost immediately, the same still, small voice spoke back to him.

"Kevin, that word was from Me."

This didn't quite line up with Kevin's theology. After all, hadn't the word been *wrong*?

Then the Lord taught Kevin a valuable lesson.

"Kevin, I wanted to show you that this is not about a performance. I'm not interested in performance, I'm interested in faith. You stepped out in faith, and as far as I'm concerned, what you did was a total success."

We're all guilty of it. Someone close to us is sick. Others are gathered around to pray for them. We step up to pray, and we are immediately faced with a line in the sand. Do we go for it and pray for total healing right then and there? Or do we pray for strength to "deal with this," or for wisdom for the doctors or grace on the family members? Have we ever stepped out and prayed for God to just out and out heal someone, yet nothing happened? Of course. Happens all the time.

Does that mean God's not listening to us? Are we doing something wrong? Later I'll deal with why I believe God doesn't heal everyone all the time; but for now, let's worry about ourselves for a moment. We have been called to be like Jesus. Our very name, Christian, refers to us as "little Christ." Jesus set an example for us when He was here, and not once did He shy away from someone who needed Him because He was intimidated. Neither should we.

I find myself falling into the trap of sometimes wanting to protect God from Himself. I realize that I'm dealing with an invisible entity here, and no matter how much I have seen or experienced, it still stretches me to step out and pray for someone to be healed—deep down I'm wondering if I'm just praying to my own imagination. I've prayed for people so often where nothing happened that when I'm faced with a situation of real need and desperation, I get nervous that once again I'm going to pray and nothing will happen, and this need and desperation in front of me is going to turn into bitterness and defeat. I don't want to subject this person to that, so I will withdraw my own bold faith and fall back on the safer, "comfort this person" prayer.

I think this reasoning is birthed from my own stupid assertion that I really have something to do with anything supernatural that is or is not happening. What I have begun to learn in my travels, though, is that in the end, it's not really about me at all. Let me give you two stories to illustrate my point.

JUST LET ME WATCH

Occasionally when I go out to film, I get sucked into what is going on and am sometimes even asked to "partake" in what is happening. My natural inclinations are, like many Christians, to stand on the sidelines and watch. I am as edified as anyone by what I'm seeing, and I'd like to keep it that way as much as possible—just let me watch. When people turn to me and say, "OK, now it's your turn," I break into a cold sweat and search for excuses why I couldn't possibly do such a thing. Nothing, it seems, is more terrifying than having to see whether or not what you say you believe is actually true or not. I may have traveled the world and have seen some of the most amazing things God has done, but when I'm the one at the center of what is happening, suddenly my faith becomes small and filled with doubt.

There was one time, though, when I was filming someone and the exact opposite was true. I was at Yale University with Jason Westerfield, and we were finishing a long, productive day of filming on the streets. I was still coming off my buzz from having seen into the supernatural realm earlier that day, and part of me didn't want this day to end, knowing that tomorrow life would return to normal.

It was around 11 at night, and we were heading back to our car when a homeless man approached us. I watched him walk up to us, limping, and my natural reflex was to look away and act like I didn't see him. The less fortunate always make us uncomfortable it seems, probably because they are such a stark reminder of just how fortunate we are in comparison. But this guy approached us with a purpose.

He timidly asked if we had any change so he could get something to eat. He was about as stereotypical as a homeless man could get. He smelled horrible, mumbled as he spoke, wouldn't look us in the eyes, and was incredibly dirty. Jason didn't miss a beat. He told the guy that sure, we'd give him some money, but first he wanted to give him something better. He then asked if he had any pain in his body, and the man told us about the pain in his neck, as well as in his leg. Jason explained to him that he was God's son, that God loved him, and that we'd like to pray for God to touch him.

The next moment will forever be burned into my memory. Jason and I gathered around this man and prayed for his leg, and I remember looking up at him through my camera view-finder, and I just stared at his face. He had a look that oozed childlike innocence. Here was a man who was normally ignored by the world. Just minutes before I was planning to ignore him too! But here he stood, right in front of me, and he didn't know what was going to happen. I had no idea what he was thinking at that moment, but I sure knew what I was thinking. This guy is about to be healed. His leg is going to be healed right here, right now. There was no shadow of doubt in my mind that this would happen.

Even when I was in the bush of Mozambique with Heidi Baker and people were being healed all around me, I still had that twinge of doubt when the next person approached, and I wondered if it would actually happen this time. But here, as midnight approached on this street outside Yale University, I knew a healing was about to happen. I would have staked my entire life on it. It was something I had never felt before, nor have I ever felt it again. At that moment, that still, small voice I had begun to hear more regularly spoke to me and said, "You are filming the end of your movie."

Jason finished praying and the man said his leg felt better. Jason asked him to run down the street and back, and upon his return, the man was smiling. He had just been healed, and he knew it. I knew it. The man was so happy, in fact, that he completely forgot to ask for the money he had originally approached us for. He walked away from us—no, he *strutted* away from us—like a man who had just been hugged by his long lost father. This was the scene that indeed did form the ending of *Finger of God,* and it is the reason I held that particular shot for so long and faded the focus on the street and traffic lights the way that I did in the finished film. I knew I was filming the end of my movie, even though I still had close to a year of shooting left to go.

TRIUMPHS AND DEFEATS

If the streets of Yale were my greatest triumph of faith, the villages of Tanzania were my shameful low point of belief. I was now filming *Furious Love,* and I had come to Tanzania to help Jeff Jansen film his crusade. His main camera person was a former student of mine, and we worked out a deal where my crew and I would come and help Jeff with his crusade if we could use whatever we filmed for my new movie. I had little idea of what to expect, but as usual, God had a few tricks up His sleeve.

One day, some of the local church leaders decided to take some members of Jeff's team up a mountain to a few remote villages for some street evangelism. I was back in my wheelhouse, and I eagerly joined them to capture whatever God had planned for these unsuspecting villagers. My technical director, Braden, was with me, and we were milling around the crowd that had gathered to hear the team speak. They all began praying for people, and I quickly noticed one of the team, Anton, praying for a villager's leg. He would pray, then ask if the man's leg was any better. The interpreter would tell him that, no, it's not better in the slightest. Anton kept praying, but nothing was happening. While I was filming this scene, Anton stood up, turned to me and said, "Hey Darren, you want to pray for him too?"

My first (and only) thought was, "No!" That was just about the last thing I wanted to do. Anton and the other team members were old hands at this stuff, had gone on countless mission trips and evangelistic outreaches, had prayed for hundreds, if not thousands of people for healing, and had preached for years and years. I had traveled the world, yes, but with a camera in my hand. I documented this stuff, I didn't actually *do* it. A large lump formed in my throat.

"Yeah...yeah...," was my response. It was about as uninspired as you can get.

I handed my camera to Braden, trading him a silent, "get me out of here" glance, then turned to meet my humiliation. I knelt down and put my hand on the man's leg. Suddenly I realized that I had no idea what to do. I had seen people pray for healing before, but I'd never actually done it myself. What was I supposed to say? What was I supposed to do? I quickly tried to remember key words or phrases I had heard people say while I was filming them, but nothing was coming to me.

I think I muttered a few lame "God, heal him," petitions, and the rest of the time I just sat there, staring at his leg, wondering how long this charade would have to continue before I would be allowed to stand up again and still make this guy feel like I had put forth some kind of an effort. I even remember thinking about the absurdity of this situation, that I was actually thinking these things. All the while, the camera was burning a hole in my back. I made a silent vow to myself that my wife would *not* be seeing this footage when I got home. How embarrassing.

Finally I stood up and turned to my interpreter. It's not that I had little faith, I had absolutely no faith that this guy had been healed. I asked him, mostly out of duty and because that seems to be the way these things are done, if the man could feel any difference. He talked to the guy, who moved his leg around a bit, put weight on it, and tested it. They talked for a while in their language, then the interpreter turned to me and said, "It's well."

What?

"It's well. He says it feels good."

I looked at the man I had just prayed for. He was smiling. It took a second for everything to register in my brain. How could this be possible? I thought you had to have some faith to heal someone. I didn't just have a little faith, I had no faith whatsoever! The only response I could muster was an incredulous, "Praise Jesus!" and I hugged the guy. It was then that I realized that this whole scene wasn't about me at all. It was about God doing what He wanted to do all along. He didn't heal the guy while Anton prayed for him because He wanted all the glory. I step in, a complete numbskull in a situation like this, pray with no faith at all, and God heals the man. When I put this experience up next to my experience with the homeless man at Yale University, one thing becomes crystal clear.

I had nothing to do with either of these miracles.

Sure God had used me, in a sense, but the healing didn't come because of my great faith or theological training. I didn't have a special gifting or use a particular formula. For one healing I had great faith, and for the other I had none. But God moved both times. How could I reconcile this?

In the end, fear is the great motivator for doing nothing for Christ. How often do I hear that inner voice, the Holy

Spirit, nudging me to step out of my comfort zone and do something, or say something to someone? How often do I ignore it? Create an excuse? Or just out and out rebel against it? I don't think God is as concerned with our results as He is with our motivation. Are we motivated to pray out of love? Fear? Glory? Fame? Curiosity? Are we motivated by performance or faith?

When we pray for someone, love must reign supreme. We cannot love them with the agenda to convert them. That is no different from my wife showering me with kisses with the hidden hope that I will buy her a new dress. That's not love; it's manipulation. But God approaches all of us, whether we believe in Him or not, with pure, agenda-less love. Our job is to simply identify a need, then step out of our own fear and into the obedience of prayer.

Let God do the rest.

Chapter 6

THE PROBLEM WITH SUPERSTARS

Hero worship is part of the very fabric of our society. Whether it comes in the form of athletes, politicians, singers, or actors, Americans have always had a thing for celebrities. Why we listen to them outside their areas of expertise is beyond me. For the life of me I can't figure out why I should allow Charles Barkley's views on American foreign policy to affect my worldview. Celebrity status is a simple concept— a lot of people know who a certain person is. Suddenly that person becomes "special" in the sense that more people are listening to him or her, and it seems like you sort of know the person. Because so many people know the celebrity, when he or she speaks, by definition, many people hear.

What does this have to do with anything? you might be wondering? While I understand and accept the fact that the world wants to create celebrities to fulfill our voyeuristic tendencies,

I wholeheartedly reject the notion of Christian celebrities, especially when it comes to those who are simply walking out what Jesus commanded.

In my position, I have met quite a few celebrated Charismatic leaders. Heidi Baker is perhaps the person with the brightest wattage I have encountered, and the fact that she is a kind of celebrity at all is wholly ironic considering her extreme desire to become like a child and fully entrust herself to the will of God. She has not asked for celebrity status, but her radical faith has inspired so many people that it was inevitable. Celebrity for celebrity's sake isn't bad in and of itself— like I just mentioned, on the surface it merely means that a lot of people know your name. But what concerns me is when believers take that celebrity beyond the borders of simple fame and into the land of obsessive pursuit.

An illustration will probably work best here. While filming *Finger of God,* I met up with Heidi in Switzerland for a big miracle conference she was attending. There were other big time speakers there, but as is usually the case when Heidi shows up somewhere, she's the real star of the show. In a sense, she has earned it. She has gone more radically into the world of faith in God than anyone I have ever met. Her life, and indeed the lives of thousands of children, often depends on whether or not God shows up. She has positioned herself in such a way that her ministry cannot continue without God's constant intervention and provision.

This is not a knock on Heidi, but rather an endorsement of her. I have yet to meet anyone who oozes as much love and compassion than I have seen from Heidi, and her courage and faith in her God to provide and heal a desperate people has inspired thousands. Unfortunately, this courage and faith can often turn into an idol for unscrupulous believers.

HEARTS BENT TOWARD HOPE

It was a scene straight out of a rock show. Heidi had just finished speaking in the giant arena in Switzerland, and it was time for her to move from the stage to the car that was waiting to take her back to her hotel for some much needed rest. As soon as she stepped off the stage, though, the crowd surged. Everyone clamored for her, begging, pleading for her to pray for them. Heidi lives in the world of the miraculous—indeed, she sees miracles every day in Mozambique among the orphans and the poor.

I watched as she tried to move, but was blocked on all sides by people reaching out to her, blocking her way so she might pray for them or simply hug them. Heidi's personal assistant tried in vain to break her away from this crowd; but of course Heidi is filled with compassion to an unusual degree, and she has a hard time saying no to someone asking for a touch of love. So there she was, hugging person after person, praying for them, giving them words of love and encouragement, while those around her tried to get her to move on, tried to make it clear to the crushing crowd that Heidi is only one woman, and that she needs her rest. Please, let her through. Let her rest.

But no one paid any attention to them because all eyes were fixed on Heidi. All hearts were bent toward the hope that maybe, just maybe, she would lock eyes with them and pray for them. These people were all desperate in their own way, they all needed healing, and Heidi was the person who might be able to give it to them.

But herein lies the problem. Heidi isn't the One who gives healing. It is Heidi's Father who does that. I would bet most Christians wholeheartedly agree on this point, as would nearly every person who was inching toward her that day in Switzerland. And while it is true that God ultimately provides the healing touch, the common thought among many Christians is that someone like Heidi provides them a *better chance of being touched by God.* In essence, the odds are greater if someone like her is the one who is praying.

I will be the first to recognize that certain people have been given certain "anointings" and a greater measure of gifting in certain spiritual areas. I have seen too much to deny that. But I will also be the first to say that if God desires to heal you at that moment, *anyone's* prayers will work. Just witness me praying for the man in Tanzania—me with no faith—to bear that out.

When I spend time with the men and women I film, I almost always ask them to pray for me before I depart. I want whatever God has given them for myself, so that I might be able to give it to others. But I also must deal with people calling my studio, or emailing me on a regular basis because they have to have Jason Westerfield or Heidi Baker, and no one else, pray for them. I have had people tell me with a straight face that they believe Jason Westerfield could heal them if only they could get him to pray for them.

SPIRITUAL SUPERSTAR SYNDROME

Look, I get it. People see God doing radical things through evangelists like Heidi and Jason as they step out in faith. Then they think the odds go up if someone who has a history of radical things happening is the one who must pray for them. Makes sense, really. But this spiritual superstar syndrome is a plague. What is ironic is the fact that, in a way, what I do for a living highlights people and makes them famous for what they're doing for the Lord. And it is this very thing that my spirit rebels against when I see it. Not that it helps much, but I always tell everyone I am filming that I am not there to make them famous. I'm there to make God more famous.

I think the reason this superstar syndrome is so abhorrent to me is because of the incredibly high failure rate of humans in general. Christians are not perfect (as we all well know), but typically the bigger and more famous a Christian becomes, the more we expect them to be perfect. It's as if they are our spokespeople, and as such, they need to be and act exactly as Jesus did to prove to the world that we aren't a bunch of hypocrites. When they fall, then it's big news; and for many non-Christians, it reiterates what they already think—Christians are a bunch of fakes who believe in fairy tales.

I remember talking with Heidi's assistant in Switzerland after she had finally escorted Heidi out of there and back to the hotel. It had taken a full 45 minutes to move 30 feet from the stage to the exit door, and by the time she got to the van, Heidi was exhausted. Heidi's assistant was lamenting what she was forced to witness day in and day out with Heidi. Everywhere she went, people clamored for Heidi to heal them. But Heidi wasn't the One doing the healing. The same God who works through her can work through everyone who is bold enough to step out in faith and ask their Father for a miracle. But it seemed that people were more and more becoming obsessed with getting to an individual because that individual had become their only hope.

I went back to my hotel room that evening thinking about all of this. That night while I was lying in bed wondering what was wrong with everybody, the Lord spoke gently to me. Again it was that familiar whisper that, when it came, quickly overtook all of my thoughts until it was the only thing in my mind I could hear. His words were simple, yet shot straight to my heart.

"They are sheep without a Shepherd."

Of course. How could I have missed it? Jesus Himself noted this as He saw the crowds flocking to Him, desperate and pleading. These were people without a leader, and when they finally saw one in Jesus, they came in droves, huge throngs crushing each other in their mania to get to the Man who heals. They tore through a stranger's roof, secretly stole touches of His clothing, and screamed at the top of their lungs until He couldn't ignore them anymore. This was the one time Hero worship was allowable.

But today, Jesus is again in our midst. When we see Him moving through individuals in a mighty way, we flock to them because we are so desperate for His touch, for His love, for Him to actually be a reality and not just a concept, that we lose our bearings and fool ourselves into believing that a particular man or woman is the best conduit through which God can touch us. We forget that God resides in all of us, that the Holy Spirit is no respecter of persons, and that He longs to make Himself known to and through His beautiful Bride.

Heidi Baker is not His only bride; we all are. It's why He healed through the hands of an unbelieving man in Tanzania. It's why He heals through the prayers of little children in Africa. It's why He heals through fans of the occult in Salem, Massachusetts, as seen in *Furious Love*. And it's why He wants to heal through you, and your pastor, and your sister, and your neighbor.

People often ask me what I want to accomplish through my films. The answer came to me one day while I was taking a shower. That still, small voice floated into my mind once again, and gave me a line I will never forget, which has since become my main reason for doing what I do.

"It is time for My Bride to begin putting on Her makeup. It is time for Her to become beautiful again."

When we look to particular men and women for healing or a touch from God, it is like my wife going to my best friend to find out what I think about her. Why wouldn't she just come to me? Why does she feel the need to ask my friend about my intentions for her? In her mind, who would know better how I feel about her than one who is close to me? But I want to show my wife *myself* that I am in love with her. I want to be the one she comes to. I want to be the one who gives her my greatest gifts. I wouldn't be much of a lover if I were to use my friends to give her my gifts. Instead, she must meet me face to face, and ask me for what she desires and needs herself, and I will gladly give her all that I own.

ONLY HUMAN

The final problem with creating spiritual superstars is the fact that, in the end, we are all only human. I have talked to many people who struggle with certain Christian leaders because of the way those individuals operate. They may be prideful, or arrogant, or flashy, or have some weird theological belief about fringe things, or they may have personalities that rub us the wrong way, or they may get divorced. It's not that we should simply overlook these things, but we need to remember to always look into our own hearts as well. What darkness lurks inside us?

Throughout history, God has used imperfect people to work through, often because when He wants a job done, He has to use whoever is available and willing, regardless of their pedigree or personality flaws. Christians have proven to be a pretty uptight bunch. We're the first to cannibalize our own wounded. We spend countless hours debating what to do with our fallen leaders. We demand that our leaders be perfect; but that will never happen, because those leaders were once like you and me. They are just men and women trying to do their best, and are often thrust to the forefront despite themselves. Look at me. One day I'm a simple college professor who hadn't really accomplished much of anything creatively in 30 years; then I agree to go make a movie (which, at the time, I had no idea where to even start) about crazy stuff Christians believe; and three years later, *Charisma* magazine is calling me one of the 21 Emerging Leaders of Tomorrow's Church! I'm now known as "the *Finger of God* guy" or "the *Furious Love* dude." The fact that you're reading this book right now shows the remarkable thing God has done through someone who had no plans of being where he is at this moment in history. And now is more expected of me because this platform has been thrust upon me? Of course it is.

Maybe this story will help. I understand that some people look at me as someone special because of what I do and the success of my films. I have watched as people hyperventilate in excitement when they visit my studio or even shake my hand, and it is always uncomfortable and strange to me. I cannot boast about anything I have done, because in reality I simply did what was asked of me. But one event happened to me early on that showed me the importance of this action of simple obedience.

Finger of God had been out for a few months and was gaining a decent audience when I was invited to be on Sid

Roth's television show, *It's Supernatural!* Now, Sid shoots a bunch of shows at one time to be more expeditious, and when I traveled down to Charlotte to be a part of this, it was my first time being on television. There were a number of people I didn't know, as well as my friend Jason Westerfield. We all shot our episodes and that night Sid hosted a dinner for us, after which we all retired to a room to pray for one another.

Now there is something you need to understand about me at this time. *Finger of God* was starting to take off, and me being the lone producer of a successful film, well, let's just say my financial situation was changing rapidly. I also realized that I had literally stumbled my way through making this movie. When it came time to edit the film and put it together, I remember sitting in my home office looking over 100 hours of random footage and wondering how in the world I was supposed to do this. About a year earlier a friend of mine had prayed for me and had given me a word about editing. He told me that when it was time to edit this movie, God was going to take me "into His womb and feed me intravenously." While I stared at my computer screen, I remembered that prayer. I literally had no idea what to do, so I began to pray. I reminded God that He had said He would take me into His womb, and I wasn't going to do anything until He showed me what to do.

I sat in my chair for a half an hour waiting for some idea of what to do. I literally had nothing, no idea how to begin. Then, out of nowhere, I saw a picture of my aunt and uncle, and I heard that still, small voice whisper, "make them laugh." It was as if I saw the opening two minutes of my film playing out in my mind, and I knew exactly what to do and how to put it together. I knew how to structure the opening to make people laugh and put them at ease. So I started editing and simply did what I had seen. I finished the scene, did the voiceover I had heard, then called it a day. I stopped because I had no idea what to do next. The next day, I prayed again and waited until God showed me the next section in my head again, then edited that together. I put the entire movie together like that. So not only could I take no personal credit for the things that I had filmed, I couldn't even take credit for putting the movie together!

I say all this to point out the reason behind the enormous internal struggle that was raging inside of me as I joined Sid Roth and the others in Charlotte. This accidental movie was proving very successful, and I was receiving a lot of attention and a fair amount of money as a result. And I was struggling with my success. Even my wife was unaware of how badly I was struggling with this success, and it was difficult for me to accept all this success from something God had done almost entirely Himself. How could I justify this? What should I do about it? Remember, I had never succeeded at anything creative in my life, and here I was garnering outlandish rewards from something I didn't even *want* to do in the first place! I can't tell you how many times I prayed and asked God why He chose me to make this movie. There must be a million other people who were more qualified, more talented than me, who would have done a better job than me with this film. Why me? Why me? Why did You choose me?

As we met in that little room in the hotel with the rest of Sid Roth's guests, I was a man in conflict. No one else knew. I doubt anyone even suspected. But soon it was my turn to receive prayer from the group, and I dutifully plopped down in the chair as this group of strangers began to pray for me. I wasn't expecting much.

There was a man there, I don't even know his name, I only remember that he was a pastor from Africa. But he began to pray for me, and these words boomed forth...

"You are wondering why God has chosen you for this task. You think there are a million other people more qualified to make this film than you, who could have done a better job than you, and you're wondering why God chose you for this."

Let's just say that this guy had my full attention at this point. Never before had I received a word that was literally word-for-word the very struggle I was dealing with. I sat on the edge of my seat, my soul crying out for God's thoughts on this very question—it was the deepest longing in my life at that moment, and my ears burned for the answer.

What followed changed me forever.

"This is what the Lord says. He did not choose you because you were more talented than others or because you have a greater understanding than others. No, He chose you *because you dared to say yes to the living God! You dared to do such a thing.* This is why you have been chosen."

I was thunderstruck. I was broken. I wept like a baby upon the realization that He understood the very depths of my heart, and that indeed I *wasn't* any better than anyone else. But this pastor wasn't finished. He had one more thing to add, and it was perhaps the most important part.

"The Lord also says this: *Stop asking!*"

They were the two words I needed to hear the most. I knew what He meant as soon as I heard them. The Lord was telling me, in no uncertain terms, to shut up, stop whining about undeserved success, and get to work. He had bigger plans for me, but as long as I was struggling with having been chosen, I would never be able to move forward.

From that day forward, I haven't looked back. I accepted God's blessing on my life, and I fully embraced the destiny He had for me. I would no longer apologize for anything the Lord gave me or provided for me. I will never seek riches or success, but if He chooses to bring it to me, I will use it for the advancement of His kingdom. While it is true that I have nothing to brag about in my success, I can finally know that my destiny is in full bloom because I simply said yes to the living God.

The same is true, I am certain, of our Christian leaders, and this is why we are called to worship Christ, not our leaders. Unfortunately, we too often *do* worship our leaders, and we become disillusioned with God when they fail. How absurd! Of course they are going to fail. The only One who will not fail, ever, is God.

When God decides to show up somewhere and a revival bursts forth and healings become commonplace, what do we do? Do we say, "God is doing a new thing here; let's enjoy His presence?" Or do we seek out the person who started it all, who prayed the prayer, and who contains all the frailties and sinful nature that we do? Do we get on a plane and go to where God is moving, hoping that we will be chosen to go on that stage and have *that man or woman* pray for us? Or do we go with the simple expectation that, regardless of who does or does not pray for us, we will simply go to enjoy the very presence of our Lover and will humbly ask Him to touch our lives? And will we accept what He does or does not give to us there? Will we worship Him not because of what He might do for us, but simply because of who He is?

If we are sheep, then we must not, we cannot, we will not lose sight of our Shepherd again.

Chapter 7

OVERCOMING AGENDA

It is one of the most memorable scenes from *Finger of God*. I'm in Istanbul, Turkey, filming with Georgian and Winnie Banov as they travel the country visiting various gypsy communities they have relationships with, in an attempt to show them God's love and compassion for them—the most hated people group in Europe.

At this stop, Heidi Baker had joined us (she is good friends with the Banovs), and I was quite cognizant of the fact that this was my final day of shooting for this film. At this point, I had no idea if I even had anything worthy of a feature film. (To me, this is further proof that God put the film together entirely. I didn't have a clue of what the final story would look like even as I finished filming!) As a result, I knew I was in a desperate place, and I was thankful that Heidi had shown up, because where Heidi is, typically, wild stuff happens. This isn't because she is extra special (see previous chapter), but simply because she is one of the most radically loving people I have ever met, and along with radical love comes radical events.

Heidi once told me about the moment her life changed forever. She was a struggling missionary in Mozambique, very close to burnout, and she had gone to that crazy church in Toronto in a last ditch effort to allow God to show her what she should do—whether or not she should just pack it all up and go home or keep grinding things out in the African countryside. That weekend, God plastered her to the floor of that church for days—she literally could not get up. During that time, she was allowed the opportunity to look into the eyes of the Father for three seconds. When she did, all she saw were endless rivers of love. Those three seconds gave her all the love she would need to take the nation of Mozambique for Christ.

LOVE SWEET LOVE

Of course, if you have ever contemplated giving up or looked to people like Heidi as standard bearers that no one else can live up to, I give you this humorous aside. Heidi has mentioned that she often feels so overwhelmed and so tired that she just wants to give up and move back to the States. Once, she told me, she even asked her assistant to get her an employment application for Nordstrom. "Why on earth would I do that, Heidi?" she asked. "Because I want to quit. I'll just sell shoes at Nordstrom," had been Heidi's answer. She wasn't joking. She was dead serious, and she demanded that her assistant get her an application immediately.

Thankfully, her assistant replied correctly, "Let's pray." The disaster was soon averted.

That day in Istanbul, thank goodness, Heidi had no intention of quitting, and she was walking around the gypsy village looking for people with whom to pray. I made sure to keep my distance, but I never took my eyes off her, knowing that wherever Heidi goes, stuff usually happens. Sure enough, I saw her approach a woman standing in a doorway, and I hurried over with my camera. The whole scene is played out in *Finger of God*.

The woman is blind in one eye, and Heidi wants to pray for her, but she needs an interpreter who, in this case, happens to be a Turkish pastor. A disagreement ensues as the pastor keeps trying to convert the woman, telling her that she must first convert to Christianity and then God may heal her. Heidi insists that she just wants to pray for the woman, hope that God heals her, and that her healing will lead to her faith in Christ. The woman doesn't want to accept Jesus, or "Christo" as she calls him. She believes in Allah. Heidi's frustration grows as she realizes the pastor isn't exactly translating her request as she is requesting it, and although she prays for the woman's eye, the whole situation is shrouded more in confusion for the woman than by a loving touch from her Father.

Heidi and the pastor reconvene immediately afterward, and the pastor voices his displeasure with these people and this Muslim woman, in particular. He accuses them of brainwashing, stupidity, and laments the fact that they don't even have to read the Qur'an. Heidi counters by telling him that he is to simply love them, love them, love them. Let the Father's love overtake them. The pastor counters with, "I do love her, but I want to train her."

Obviously, he missed the point on this one.

This is where things get tricky for me. I occasionally get emails from people who are mad at me for implying that what the pastor did was wrong. All he's trying to do, they say, is save that woman from eternal damnation. All that blonde lady (their words, not mine) wants to do is speak hippy love over her. I have actually had people write me and say the following words: "What good does love do anyone? What matters is the Gospel!"

I have tried to constantly watch what I say about God's people; but in this case, my patience is strained almost to the breaking point. I understand, to a point, where my critics are coming from. I understand their mindset, because it was a similar mindset to the one I used to have. Just get people saved; that's the bottom line. Everything else is gravy. Nothing else matters. Get them to sign on the dotted line and then God will love them. Then they'll have the magic ticket to get into Heaven. Then Jesus will embrace them. Until that point, they are lost creatures worthy of the full wrath of God. He doesn't acknowledge them or even particularly want them until they want Him.

Nowhere in the Scriptures, and particularly in the person of Jesus, do I see this mentality. Jesus didn't eat with "sinners" *after* they voiced their belief in Him. He ate and drank with them, embraced them, loved them in their current state. They were won over through the sheer force of His love for them. No tricks. No emotional games. No fear tactics. No agenda. He wanted to be with them because He loved them. If they chose to remain in their lives of sin after experiencing His love, that was their decision. It wouldn't affect His love for them. In the end, it was left up to them to decide.

I don't think much has changed since then. At least not on Jesus' part. We, on the other hand, have a major agenda problem.

EYE PLANKS

Let me first take the plank out of my own eye...

I was filming *Furious Love* and had just heard about a witch-craft and occult festival that occurs in Salem, Massachusetts, throughout the entire month of October. I got the bright idea of going there and "picking a fight" with the enemy. The plan was simple. Bring a couple of heavy spiritual hitters, walk the streets, and watch the fireworks ensue as the demonic encountered God's children of light. We were going to blow that place up (in the spiritual sense, of course). Heck, if all went well, we'd cause such a ruckus that we'd make the evening news. No matter what, we'd get some spectacular footage for this film of ours.

I called Jason Westerfield and asked him if he was open to going with me. He mentioned that he'd love to, and had actually been there a few years earlier. He said it was awesome; healings and salvations had broken out all over the place the last time he was there. Sweet, I thought. We're going to be the devil's worst nightmare this October.

My new friend, Will Hart, who would soon accompany us to Thailand, had family in the area, so he agreed to join us as well. I had my dream team set, and we flew into Boston ready to rock the world. I had set up an interview with a major witch in the area, and I was wondering how God was going to show who the Boss was during that encounter. I went to a bookstore that evening to kill time and received a phone call from Will.

"Wilson, we need to talk." Will sounded serious. So unlike him. "I just got a call from Ravi."

A little back story. Will would soon introduce me to his friend Ravi, who will be introduced to you shortly in another chapter. Ravi has a gift unlike any I have ever seen. Since he became a believer at the age of 17, Ravi hears the audible voice of God—every day. More on him later. But for now, let it be known that he had just called Will and they'd had the following conversation. (Ravi knew nothing about what we were doing, by the way. All he knew ahead of time was what Will had told him—that he was going to be filming with me and he would be visiting his parent's house.)

"Will, what are you doing?" Ravi had asked Will.

"What do you mean?"

"What are you doing tomorrow?"

"I'm going to film with Darren," Will replied, perplexed.

"You're going to be speaking with a witch tomorrow, aren't you?"

Will nearly dropped the phone. How did Ravi know this? Oh yeah…. "Yes," he said, tentatively.

"Don't do it. What you think will happen will not happen. Daddy doesn't want you to waste your time; plus, this man is not someone you should interview. But the Lord also wants you to know that He will be with you, and some amazing things are going to happen tomorrow."

Will knew Ravi well enough to realize when he should listen, and he immediately called me to tell me what Ravi had told him. I was, obviously, dumbfounded by the circumstances (and I secretly couldn't wait to meet Ravi myself), and

I too understood that the Lord was clearly rearranging our schedule. I was also immensely relieved to hear that God not only knew where we were and what we were up to, but also that He was with us. This fact would become our rock in our future travels as we stepped into darker territory. But for now, God was making clear to me what He *didn't* want us to do.

The next morning we showed up at the festival bright and early. We enjoyed our morning coffee, interviewed a local pastor in the area, planned our assault, and began walking around. The beginning of any street filming we do is always a little awkward, since you're stepping out in faith and trying to garner the courage to actually *do* what you've been talking about doing for months. We were here for two days only, and we were confident that God would show up like He always does. But it always feels kind of weird to be walking around with video cameras.

Actually, I should back up. We didn't start walking around. My *crew* began walking with Will. Meanwhile, I was to shadow Jason, and for the moment, Jason wasn't going any-where. He stood as still as a statue, right in the middle of this place, and prayed.

I am constantly shamed by the people I meet. When you make movies for God and hear all the praise that people heap on you—about how their lives have been radically changed forever because of *your faithfulness* or *your movie* or what-ever—it's easy to grow a little complacent and more than a little content with yourself. *They're right,* I'll tell myself. *I'm a pretty amazing Christian.* But then God puts me on a plane and I meet people like Jason Westerfield, or Ravi, or Philip Mantofa, and I am once again reminded, sometimes in a great spasm of self-reproach, that I'm actually a pretty lousy

Christian. These people scattered around the world are the real heroes. I'm just a recorder. And a fairly hypocritical one at that.

THE WITCHCRAFT FESTIVAL

I bring this up because on this particularly crisp fall day in October, Jason stood in the middle of a witchcraft festival and prayed. But this wasn't like the perfunctory prayers I had been used to praying my whole life, when my friends and I would get together and quickly ask God to bless our time or show us what to do, or some other equally rushed and hurried prayer that was merely meant as the prelude to the real show: us doing our thing. No, this was a prayer of a patient man whose entire life is built on prayer. He just stood there, unmoving, waiting on his Father to show him what to do. I have no idea what he was asking, but I do know that I sat there like a bump on a log for over an hour. Some people noticed him, but most just passed on by, figuring he was another free-spirited whack-job who was drawn to places like this.

Later, I asked him what took so long. He gave me an interesting response.

"Look, we can do this one of two ways: 1) I can do it shotgun style, where I pray for anyone who suits our fancy. Some will get blasted, while others won't feel a thing. If that's what you want to do, we can do that. It's your movie. Or 2), we can try to be a little more effective and find out what the Father is up to, what He wants us to do. That way, our success rate goes way up."

Once again I felt like a flea. Here Jason was just trying to take the position that Jesus took, to "only do what my Father is doing" (see John 5:19), and I was getting frustrated because my camera was feeling heavy. You'd think I'd have learned my lesson by now.

In my defense, I was more than a little confused once we got started. Jason would occasionally approach random strangers whom God had seemingly highlighted to him, but when he would pray for them, nothing would happen. Just as it would soon happen to Will when we went to Thailand, Jason was beginning to get flustered because he could *feel* the presence of God, and he *knew* he was praying for whom he was supposed to pray, yet nothing was happening. As he put it to me with more than a little frustration in his voice, "I know God is here and that He wants to heal, but for some reason He's not releasing anything."

By that evening, it was becoming apparent that something was obviously wrong with our approach. Will and my crew hadn't had any success, and this was the first time I had ever seen Jason getting completely shut out. Our approach had been simple: follow Will and Jason at a distance, film while they prayed, and hopefully something would happen. We were sneaking around, just as I had done many times before, but this time nothing was happening. Could this have been one giant mistake? Where was my fight? Where were all the manifestations? The fireworks? I had just spent thousands of dollars to make this happen, and now it looked like I had been a total idiot. I will freely admit it now. I was about as nervous as I have ever been on a shoot, when we took a break to go out for dinner.

We tried to go to a nice seafood place, but the wait was too long, so we meandered over to an incredibly greasy fried food restaurant that we'd all certainly regret in the morning. Jason approached me on the way to the grease pit and asked me a question that would change everything from that moment on.

"Dude, what are you doing here?"

It took me by surprise, but I answered as best I could.

"Trying to make a movie."

"No, that's not what I mean. What are you doing *here*? Why did you come here, to this place to film?"

I thought for a moment.

"Because there's a witchcraft festival here."

"Exactly," he said, "what we've been doing, we can do anywhere. We don't need to come to Salem to do this. We could be filming in Chicago, or Connecticut, or anywhere really if all we're going to do is what we've already done before."

I knew he was right, and my heart sank even further as I realized we were all getting on a plane tomorrow morning and I had just had my first, horrendous failure. Had I even asked God what He wanted us to do? I had come with a locked-and-loaded agenda to pick a fight and film people being overpowered by my Superhero God. Jason and Will were both in agreement that His presence was with us, that He wanted us to be here, but whatever we were doing was wrong. We needed a new approach, and fast.

So we chugged our milkshakes and stared at each other, wondering what to do. It was my brother-in-law, Matt, who threw it out there first.

"We've been sneaking around all day. Why don't we just make a spectacle of ourselves? Put the cameras up right in the middle of the festival and invite people to come to us. Tell them we'll give them free "spiritual cleansings" or something. Just get 'em to sign up to let Jason pray for them."

As soon as he said it, something leapt inside my spirit. It was more than just hope at a new idea (others were brandishing other ideas as well), but there was something about *this* particular idea that resonated with me. I had no idea what would happen, nor was I entirely sure this is what God wanted us to do. But my spirit yearned for us to do this, and I was a desperate man. I had made *Finger of God* by myself, and I had never considered myself a director before, mostly because I just stumbled through making that movie. But here, inside this funky little restaurant, five people were staring at me (Jason's assistant had joined us), waiting for me to make a decision. I was the director; it was my call. They were all here because I had invited them. They were here to do whatever I asked them to do. I was supposed to be the one making God's movie, and I was supposed to know what God wanted us to do. My nerves were shot, my blood pressure was peaking, and I was scared to death that it had all been a waste.

LET'S DO IT!

All I knew for sure was that what we were doing wasn't working. I had a sense this new plan was the way to go, but it wasn't much of a sense. Just a feeling in my gut. But that could simply be the greasy fried fish I had just eaten. No time to think any longer. Decision time.

"Let's do it."

We had a plan, and somehow that eased the tension for everyone. I know no one blamed me, but we were all staring at a major fiasco here, and no one wanted that. We hatched the plot as we drove back to the festival. Matt and Will would fish for people and explain what we were doing, since they were the most outgoing and approachable. Jason's assistant would take care of the release forms. Braden and I would film. Jason would pray. We had new vigor as we set up the cameras. It was around 8 in the evening, and time was slipping away. The festival would close up shop soon.

We were ready to roll when Jason asked us all to gather together to pray. Again, I was ready for a perfunctory "God, show up" prayer, and then we'd get to work doing His will. But Jason began praying, and he didn't stop. I mean it, he didn't stop. For, like, 45 minutes, there we were, five guys huddled together next to a funnel cake vendor, looking like we were coming up with a play to win a football game. At first I was all into it. Yeah, let's pray. We've done every-thing wrong so far, best to pray. Definitely. But then as the clock kept ticking and Jason wouldn't shut up, I began to grow nervous, and then outright upset that this was taking so long.

Seriously, did we need to pray *this* long? Didn't God know what we were up to? Didn't He say He was with us? Didn't He say great things would happen while we were here? Didn't Jason know what *time* it was? The others, I could tell, were thinking the same thing. I sneaked a peak at Matt, and he shot me a look like, "What the heck?" But Jason persisted; he was not to be deterred. He was waiting for something, that was obvious, but I feared this Charismatic feeling-around-in-the-spirit stuff was going to ruin my movie. I wanted to inter-rupt, I should have interrupted, but something held me back. It was like I was defenseless against this prayer. It would have been the most shameful act in my life to interrupt this prayer. At least that's what it felt like.

By the time he finally said, "Amen," I was positive there wouldn't be anyone left for whom to pray. It was nearly 9 P.M., and the crowd had thinned considerably. Matt and Will went right to work, as anxious by the length of that prayer as I was, and soon they had snagged a few people who had seen our cameras and wondered what was going on.

A movie, you say? Some guy's going to pray for me who may know stuff about me no one else knows? I may *feel* stuff? It's free? "Sign me up!" was the general reaction we got. One thing I learned about those interested in witchcraft over these last two days was that, regardless of anything else, these people were interested in an *experience*. They wanted to see and feel something. They wanted to know that the power they served was real. Soon we had a waiting list of people who had been waiting for nearly 45 minutes for this experience, and I thought about what the reaction might be if I had tried to do this at an evangelical Christian gathering. Would people be so eager to be part of this? Based on the emails I often received, I wasn't so sure. But here we were, and there was no going back. Jason began praying for people, and I held my camera at the ready, filming it all, waiting with baited breath to see what kinds of manifestations were about to take place. The fight was on, and I didn't have to hide my camera anymore.

BETTER THAN ANY PSYCHIC

What happened over the next two hours is a little hard to explain. More than anything, I received an education. Will and Matt had the privilege of talking to the people after Jason had prayed for them, and they reported to me afterward that every person told them that was one of the craziest things they'd ever experienced. Almost all of them had gone to psychics before, but Jason, they said, was better than any psychic they'd ever been to. He knew more than vague stuff about them, he knew the very longing of their hearts. He knew their personalities.

Of course, it wasn't Jason who knew these things—it was their Father who created them. He was simply whispering in Jason's ear. Many were profoundly affected.

I was standing right next to all of them, and with each prayer a light grew brighter in my heart. How could I have missed it? What a fool I had been. When Jason was praying for the practicing witch, an encounter highlighted in *Furious Love,* that familiar whisper floated into my mind, a voice I knew well, yet never failed to doubt when I heard it. But this time, there was no doubt. I knew my Father was talking to me.

"Do you see?" I heard Him speak, "I didn't come to pick a fight. I came to love."

Occasionally while I am filming, the Lord speaks like this to me. Each time He does, I know what I am filming is going to show up in the finished film, one way or another. He spoke when I filmed the homeless man at the end of *Finger of God.* He spoke to me at the New Age festival that is featured at the end of *Furious Love* (He actually spoke the final words of the movie to me there—and I knew I had just filmed the ending). And He was speaking now, and it was, in every sense, a Father with His arm around His young son, showing him one of His most precious secrets.

This was a moment for a lifetime, a moment that would not just change my film, but would change the very fabric of my life forever. God's love suddenly became more than a concept. It became more than just an attachment to a theological argument. It became real. Potent. Alive. It was a love not just for me, but for the entire world.

GOD'S AGENDA—LOVE

When I arrived in Salem, my agenda was clear and open for everyone to see. I told my crew what we were there for, to pick a fight in Jesus' name. By the time I boarded the plane home, my agenda had been shattered and replaced by a new theology. A theology of love. God is not interested in fighting us, although He will allow us to pound away at Him in our own brokenness and fear. He will not lash out at us for our cold hearts or our hypocrisy. He does not have an agenda when He approaches us, except to ravish us with His love. He does not say, "If you do this, or accept this truth, or call Me Lord, then I will love you."

Not once in the entire time that Jason prayed for those people did God give them an ultimatum. Instead, He marked them with His love. Whether or not they acted on that touch was entirely up to them, but God's love for them, well, in that they had no choice. He was going to love them regardless of them loving Him back, or even believing in Him. There would obviously be consequences for their rejection, but in this life, God was willing to spend their entire existence pursuing, chasing, and running after them. Just as He has committed to doing with you.

Christians, I think, have a terrible habit of viewing people as projects. Our desire to "get people saved" often supersedes our biblical mandate to *love the Lord your God with all your heart and with all your soul and with all your strength and with all your mind, and your neighbor as yourself*" (Luke 10:27). I used to think that the greatest love I could show someone was found in proving to them that they needed to become a Christian, in converting them. But I had a pretty lousy concept of what salvation entailed. If I'm supposed to love my neighbor as myself, that means I need to treat them like I want to be treated. I don't know about you, but I don't want to be converted. When I get in a theological argument with someone, there's no way they're going to "convert" me to their way of thinking, especially if I think I'm right.

Why would our neighbor be any different? Who wants to be converted, or worse, viewed as someone who needs conversion? I am not your project, and for you to think I am is highly offensive.

But I do want to be loved. Go ahead and disagree with me; you wouldn't be the first person. Go ahead and think I'm crazy for actually believing that God maybe does put gold teeth in people's mouths. But if you approach me with the attitude that I am a sinner for believing such nonsense and that you are the person designated to set me straight, then I'm going to be about as defensive as I can get with you. You will not penetrate my mind or my spirit. I will keep you at bay, because I know for a fact that you don't give a rip about me. You just want to be proved right.

Instead, try loving me. Try putting yourself in my shoes. Understand what I have gone through to get to this point. Have a little empathy. A little compassion. Suspend your judgment for a minute and understand *who I am*. Don't approach me with an agenda. Approach me with an olive branch. Approach me as your brother. Do that, and don't be surprised by how much I may let you in.

God has called us to go out and make disciples of all nations, not converts. A disciple implies a personal relationship, and all good relationships start with the core understanding that the other person does, in fact, love us and is looking out for our best interests.

It is my contention that maybe, just maybe, we need to lay our agendas down, both as individual Christians and as a Church as a whole, and simply begin loving those around us, those in need, with no strings attached. What would this world look like if we simply let the force of His grace and mercy and character win them over?

Chapter 8

PURITY IN AN AIRPORT

Philip Mantofa is a treasure to the world. I'm not usually known for gushing about a particular person, simply because I fear it feeds into the superhero syndrome within the church, but in Philip's case I make an exception. This guy is the real deal, and he reminds me of a kind of prototype of what Christians are supposed to look and act like. He, of course, would blush at such a description, and he would be the first to downplay it and say that no, he's just a man who sins right along with the rest of us, and that is precisely why I love him so much. Philip operates in a level of healing and miracles and love that is far beyond almost anyone I have ever met. He has stories of the supernatural that would make your head spin, yet he is as humble and unassuming as anyone I know.

In 2008, I planned on going to Indonesia to film an event titled The Call. It was basically a giant gathering of Christian youth who met for a day to repent and pray for their country. Since I was going to be in that area of the world anyway, I started asking around if there was anyone else in the neighborhood I should meet and possibly film for *Furious Love*. A friend of mine then told me to call a guy by the name of Jaeson Ma, in LA, who apparently knew *everyone* in Asia (a gross exaggeration, obviously, but you get the point). So I called and asked him who he might suggest for me to film.

He started naming a bunch of people I had never heard of, and told me a little about their ministries, but with each passing name, nothing captured my heart, and I started to wonder if God just wanted us to go to this Call thing and that's it. But then he mentioned Philip Mantofa. I can't even remember what he told me about him initially, but the moment I heard his name, I perked up. It was as if something in my spirit surged when I heard this name, and I talked with Jaeson for about ten minutes about this Philip character. By the time I hung up, I knew I had to meet him, yet I didn't know why. I made a connection with Philip through Jaeson, and we set up a few days when I'd visit Surabaya, Indonesia, to film with him and his church.

I knew very little about him, other than he was my age, was the head pastor of a gigantic church of 30,000 people, and that Jaeson couldn't stop gushing about him. I looked forward to meeting him, but he was a side trip, a secondary stop in our real goal: to film The Call. I was told there would be over 100,000 young people at this event, and the thought of filming that kind of a gathering made my crew salivate.

About a week before we were set to fly to Indonesia (which turned out to be, by far, the most expensive trip in all of *Furious Love's* filming), I still had no idea what exactly I was going to be filming most of the time. Between getting my crew there, travel costs, food, lodging, etc., I was looking at a nearly $20,000 investment to film. I couldn't communicate much with the people who were heading up The Call, and Philip's wife was answering my emails, but wasn't answering any of my specific questions due to an obvious culture and language gap. One week from liftoff, and I was beginning to sweat.

WHOSE MOVIE IS IT?

I took my dog for a walk along the path next to our house, and I was upset. I felt like I was supposed to go on this trip to film, but I was becoming incredibly frustrated by not knowing what I was supposed to film. I railed at God while my dog sniffed around the yard. How am I supposed to plan properly when You won't tell me what to do? I'm spending a ton of money here, God, and I need to know it's not a wild goose chase. Nobody will answer my questions. Am I simply spending $20,000 to get 30 seconds of footage of a stadium filled with people? Can I get some answers please? I am, after all, trying to make a movie about You, God!

I think I complained a little more, when suddenly, like lightning, He spoke. I could take you today to the exact spot where it happened, because it was loud and it was profound. Nothing audible, as usual, but crystal clear. The voice inside my head sounded firm and, dare I say, annoyed.

"Whose movie is this?"

"Yours," I said out loud.

"Do you want to make this movie without Me?"

"No, of course not."

"Do you want this to be My film or your film?"

"Yours."

"Why?"

"Because I've seen what happens when I try to make stuff on my own." I was answering Him out loud. My dog ignored me, as usual.

"Who put *Finger of God* together?"

"You did."

"And how did that one turn out for you?"

I hesitated on this one. I knew He had me. Checkmate. "Really good."

"If you want Me to make this film for you, then you need to *trust Me*."

The words carried with them a note of finality. The last time I had heard Him this clearly was on the balcony of that crazy church in Toronto when He had just played catch with me. I had a feeling this was as close to audible that I might get. It was just so *loud* in my ears. I knew He had nothing more to say to me. The ball was in my court.

"OK, I trust You. Just make it clear to me eventually."

There was no answer, and I realized as soon as I said it what a stupid statement it was. Like He wouldn't make it clear to me....

MY TWIN BROTHER, PHILIP

Philip was the first stop, and as soon as I met him, I knew why we had come to Indonesia. I didn't just like this guy instantly—I loved him. He was like my long lost twin brother who just happened to be Indonesian. I was relatively short and...let's call it stocky, and he was tall and thin. While I was playing Nintendo in my room and was terrified of girls as a teenager, he had been a teenage martial arts expert. He once got jumped by nine men in a hotel room and beat them all up by himself. I once stubbed my toe really badly. He had seen demons in his house. I had watched scary movies a couple of times. Despite our differences, we were, and still are, brothers. He even introduced me to his church of 30,000 people as his twin brother.

But my reason for coming wasn't just to make a new friend; it was to teach me, and I believe the Western church, a lesson. I have yet to meet anyone on the planet more obsessed with holiness than Philip. In Indonesia and much of Asia, Philip is a *really* big deal. He's like an Asian Benny Hinn if you need a comparison. But he lives humbly. He told me his main goal in life is to earn the right to call the Holy Spirit by His first name. To have that right, to know the Spirit on an intimate basis, he first must become holy.

But Philip is about more than making good decisions in life. The dude carries a big spiritual stick as well.

How about this one.

Philip told me a story about a time he came home from a particularly long time of ministering at a conference six hours away. He finished preaching, prayed for about a zillion people, then immediately got into his car and commuted the six hours back to his house. By the time he arrived he was nearly sleep-walking. He knew the house was empty. He stepped out of his car and trudged through his front door.

As soon as he closed the door behind him, he saw them. Two figures stood in his living room, and they spoke to one another in low, hushed tones. He immediately knew they were demons, but he was so tired at this point that he hardly cared. Had his family been home, it would have been a different story, but since it was just him, he knew he was safe, and he ignored them as he went into his bedroom and threw his suitcase in the corner. Once in his bedroom, he heard them speak.

"He's home. Let's kill him."

He hadn't even undressed, but just fell onto his bed with his clothes on, exhausted. He opened his eyes and saw that the two demons had entered his bedroom and were now right in front of him. One was a big, muscular demon and the other was a giant, over 9 feet tall. Both were ugly. They were clearly trying to murder him. Then Philip did something that I simply cannot comprehend. He told them, quite simply, that he was very tired and he didn't have time to deal with them. He then immediately fell asleep.

Philip was telling me this story in the car as we drove somewhere, and I stopped him at this point and demanded he explain himself.

"So Philip, you're telling me that two demons are in your house, say 'there he is, let's kill him,' and you are able to lay down and go to sleep? How is that possible?"

Philip didn't quite know what to say. I knew he wasn't pulling my leg. His face betrayed no air of superiority or any of the common tells of some people I had met or interviewed who were obviously pushing the truth a little. Instead, I was staring at a man who was frustrated that he couldn't help me understand his mentality. I learned later that he hesitates to tell some of these stories because he fears that people will view him as special or as some kind of spiritual superhero. That is the last thing he wants. He is just a man, as he is fond of reminding me. Just a man.

He elaborated. If someone is demon possessed or is being attacked by the devil, he will not sleep until every last demon is gone. If his family is in danger, he will fight until he passes out. But if it's just him, well, he doesn't worry about that. He knows he's protected by a power higher and greater than all others.

I still couldn't fathom doing that. He and I may be a lot alike, but certainly not in *that* department.

He told me when he awoke, his pillow had been shredded to pieces just inches from his face. There were feathers everywhere, and it looked as if a wild animal had been trying to claw his face off but had only been able to get within a few inches of his face. That's a new one, he thought. Why did they have to destroy his favorite pillow?

He later told me that he wouldn't advise too many people to desire this, but he actually wants them to come back. I asked him why in the world he would want such a thing, and he told me he does for two reasons. If he ever meets them again, he will first demand that they release whoever they are holding in bondage. Then he is going to demand that they go out and find him a new pillow as good as the one they destroyed. Because of what they did, he had to spend his valuable time getting a new pillow, and he wasn't about to let them get away with that. He had a score to settle with them. And they would do it too, because he is the son of the King.

SON OF THE KING

This was a phrase Philip was fond of saying whenever I asked him about some crazy story he would tell me. He once told me about a time he was driving somewhere in Surabaya, and he passed a particular club that was well-known for the debauchery and evil that happened there. His spirit became enraged, and he spoke out loud, "By tomorrow, you will be destroyed!"

The next morning he opened the newspaper and discovered that the very club had burned down during the night. I asked him if the Lord had told him to make that proclamation, and he looked at me with an odd look in his eyes, as if I had asked another one of my fairly stupid questions.

"My brother," he reminded me yet again, "I'm the son of the King. My Father listens to me when I speak."

By the time I left Philip, I understood what he was trying to tell me. He wasn't saying this out of any kind of pride or belief that he was more special than anyone else. He was simply stating a fact. He fully understood who he was, and more importantly, who his Father is. As long as he said something that lined up with the will and heart of his Father, it had to happen. His Father listens to His son because He loves His son. In Philip's case, I also discovered, God trusts His son. This was the second part of the puzzle. It is one thing to receive God's love; it is quite another to earn His trust.

Philip revealed two examples of his pursuit of holiness and relationship with God at all cost, which in turn allowed God to trust His boy with unprecedented experiences and authority. The first came when God spoke to him, audibly, and asked him to do something quite difficult.

Philip became a believer in Christ in his late teens. He was dabbling in the occult at the time, as well as in the spiritual side of martial arts, and he had spent most of his life running from God. He attended a church service, and as the preacher began the altar call, Philip stood to leave. Enough of this garbage. But as he reached the back door, he heard an audible voice speak to him. It told him if he left now, he was on his own forever.

Philip turned around and no one was there. That's when the altar call was given, and Philip ran to the front of the church. He was the only one there, and almost immediately, a white light exploded in the church and blinded him from everyone around him. The voice spoke to him again and said, "I am Jesus and I love you, Philip." He realizes he must have looked like a crazy person to the entire church by his reaction, which was uncontrollable weeping and repentance. But he didn't care. He'd just been marked by God's love, and there was no turning back.

Philip stepped into the faith with both feet. He never went anywhere without his Bible—he even slept with it. He prayed for hours every day. He became a Jesus junkie.

When the Lord gave him His request, Philip saw incredible miracles happening on a regular basis whenever he laid hands on someone and prayed for them.

One afternoon, Philip was spending time with the Lord in his laundry room (this was the place he could get the most privacy!). The Lord gave him an "open vision," which is simply a vision seen in the natural with your own two eyes. This isn't something you see in your mind or imagination; it is as real as any reality you know. He saw the Person of Father God on His throne, and He was very close to Philip, right there in his laundry room! He spoke to Philip very politely, and there was no demanding tone in His voice at all. He simply revealed His desire for Philip, and that desire was for Philip to return to Him the healing gift that Philip had been operating in.

God told Philip that He just wanted Philip by His side, and to leave that job to someone else, one of His servants.

It was very much a choice, but for Philip, the right choice was obvious. Although he was greatly saddened to separate with this gift, he told the Lord that his love for Him was greater than his sadness for giving it up. In essence, Philip chose God's presence over God's gifts.

When he gave it back to God, the gift of healing vanished for 12 years. In its place, though, was a strong and profound presence of God and His Spirit both in and around Philip that has continued ever since. Later, in 2004, the gift was returned, as Philip puts it, "in style and with full-blown interest" when thousands were miraculously healed in one night when Philip spoke, without him laying a hand on anyone. For Philip, it has been history from then on.

The other story that Philip told me was in reference to something that happened between him and God, and it is a story of extremes. Philip is, in a sense, a man of extremes. It just so happens that his extremes are for holiness and purity. I am always challenged by this guy.

It was at a time when he and his wife had very little money. He was heading home from a revival meeting in Brunei Darussalam, but he had left his credit card at home with his wife. At the service before he left, he felt the Lord telling him to put his biggest bill in the offering, which he obediently did. He admitted to me that had he known what was about to happen, he would have split the large bill up into much smaller ones!

On his flight home, he had nearly a day-long layover in Kuala Lumpur. At that time, the airlines gave out vouchers for hotel stays for layovers of that length. Philip is fond of saying that when he flies somewhere, he doesn't pray before the plane takes off, like most people do. Instead, he prays when he lands, that God would guide his footsteps and would preserve his holiness. He went to the hotel kiosk and looked up the hotel he had been given a voucher for. While all the other hotels in the vicinity touted their comfortable beds or fine cuisine, this particular hotel flaunted its wild nightlife. Philip instantly had a bad feeling about this place. He decided that he would not stay at this hotel, but would spend the night in the airport.

Philip called his wife and told her what happened and then exclaimed that he would not be staying in this hotel tonight. His wife begged him to reconsider. She knew he was tired, that he'd just preached for weeks, and that he had no other options. "Where would you go?" she asked him. He told her he'd just sleep in the airport. She tried everything she could to change his mind. She trusted him. He had never even glanced at another woman when they were together, so she knew he wouldn't do anything. But Philip was adamant. He would not stay there.

I wondered, did he fear his own weakness?

"No. I knew I would not watch or do anything bad."

Then why not just stay there? Unplug the television or something. Why go to such an extreme?

"I have children. If there was a truck barreling down the road, I would not allow my children to even go near it because I love them so much. In the same way, I do not want to put my own holiness even in the vicinity of danger."

Philip realizes who he is. He understands his position. He knows that if he ever falls into sin, there are tens of thousands of people who may fall or stray from the faith themselves because they have put their trust in him. They would grow disillusioned with Christ or with Christianity, and that is all damage that he will have caused because he did not live up to the incredible faith God has put in him. He was not about to jeopardize his testimony. He would do whatever it took to protect his Father from his own weakness.

So he stayed at the airport and had perhaps the most uncomfortable night's sleep of his life. Years later when revival broke out where he was speaking, and people were being healed, thousands were getting saved, and God was moving at an unprecedented level through Philip, the Lord spoke to him and told him then that he was seeing this breakthrough and was being given this authority because he has paid a high price for holiness.

In essence, God can trust Philip.

Can the same be said about us?

Chapter 9

FINDING THE GOOD

There I was, standing in the middle of the magnificent Cathedral of Notre Dame in Paris, France, and I was seething. I've never considered myself an idealist or even particularly emotional, but standing there, seeing what this place had become…well, let's just say I had a camera and I was going to use it to teach these money changers a lesson.

I should probably explain where this sudden outburst of anger and resentment came from. A few months before I traveled to Paris en route to filming a healing conference in Switzerland (hey, if you're going to travel, why not see the nearby sights while you're at it), I had gone to Mozambique, Africa, to film with Heidi and Rolland Baker. I had seen poverty on a grand scale, driven by homeless masses, and I had seen children roaming the streets like wild animals with no supervision, no direction, no *hope*.

I had seen a bright beacon of love in the persons of Heidi and Rolland Baker and had seen the great strides they have taken to advance the Kingdom of God through their ministry, Iris Ministries. But there was so much more to do, so many people still on the edge of oblivion, hopelessness, and lawlessness. There was so much need.

You cannot see true poverty and walk away untouched. When you see it on television, you can turn the channel, but when you walk the very streets of poverty with your own two feet, it takes on a different dimension, a different reality. It *becomes* reality.

Just as seeing the miraculous time and time again changed the reality of my own theology, so has traveling the world and seeing the lost—the truly lost, those who are lost in spirit *and* in body—changed my own understanding of how poor of a job the worldwide Church is doing. We talk often of showing the love of God to others, and we read our Bibles during our "quiet times" in our comfortable chairs, sipping our coffee, and we allow ourselves to skim over the tough sections—the ones that talk about being a light in a lost world, of caring for the widows and the orphans and the poor. That is not our world, we tell ourselves. We haven't been called to that.

If you live on this planet, that *is* your world. That *is* your reality. Just as it is my reality, whether I want it or not.

My goal is not to make you feel guilty. Once again, I am chief of all hypocrites. I'm just calling it as I see it, and what I see comes from my own broken, callous heart. Jesus said that "the harvest is plentiful but the workers are few" (see Matt. 9:37). As I continuously venture into areas of the world where pain, heartache, and hopelessness are the ever present reality for all around me, I begin to see Jesus' point. All they need is hope.

All they need is peace. All they need is food. And Someone who cares about them. If the Church will not do this, who will?

This was my mindset, my new reality, as I stood in this massive monument to the majesty of God in Paris. This cathedral had been built nearly 1,000 years prior, and it is just as astonishing today as it was when it opened. I love cathedrals and the Catholic ideal of a space of worship being itself a testament to the grandeur and power of the God who created the universe. Why, then, was I so angry as I stood in the middle of the granddaddy of cathedrals in what I consider one of the greatest cities in the world? Why was I feeling so mutinous in this house of the Almighty?

Because the place had been turned into a tourist trap.

It was a Sunday, and mass was in full swing. Parishioners sat dutifully watching and listening, but around them, on all sides, stood tourists in plaid shorts and polo shirts, chomping their gum with their fanny packs hanging loosely around their waists. The click of cameras was incessant, and the chatter constant. But that wasn't even what burned me the most.

All along the sides of the cathedral are small chapel areas where people can light a candle and pray to various saints. At each stop, there is a donation box where a "suggested" amount is posted for praying there, and the price goes up depending on to whom you're going to be praying. I didn't know if I was more shocked that I was being asked to pay nearly $5 to pray to Jesus or that Jesus' wasn't the most expensive chapel in there! Crammed in the back is a little tourist gift shop selling all sorts of Cathedral-related trinkets.

Now before I offend a high church friend of mine who may be reading this, please know that I understand the basic idea. I understand that for a church like this, there is incredible overhead and a constant need for funds to keep the place in good condition, for renovations, and the like. I even get, to a point, asking for a donation if you're going to use a candle provided by the church, especially since many people won't pay a dime yet will still use a candle, which obviously costs money. I have many wonderful Catholic friends and hold no ill will or animosity toward any. We may have a few differences of opinion, but as long as you believe and love Jesus as your Lord, I will stand beside you as a brother.

FOR THE POOR

No, what really bothered me that day, and especially when placed in the context of the severe poverty from where I had just come, was the beat-up, metal box I was staring at that was attached to an enormous stone column, somewhat hidden with no lights announcing it was there.

The offering boxes to the saints were well-kept and easy to see. You couldn't miss them if you tried. But this box had obviously seen better days, and was dented in places and scratched up. On the front of the box were three words, simply stated: "For the poor."

Never before had I been so angry in a church. All around me was tourism, greed, and people who were here for the show, not for God. The gift shop was making a pretty profit that day, judging by the massive line forming, yet not one person, *not one person*, in the half-hour I stood there, had so much as noticed this little offering box, much less put any money into it. Is this what the world sees? Is this why they find it so hard to believe us when we try to get them to join our "club"? Do we appear to want money more than we want to help?

At this moment, and at this point in my life, and with those memories of poverty raging through my head, that's exactly what I was thinking. I was mad at my brothers and sisters. I was mad at Catholics. I was mad at those stupid televangelists who make us all look like crooks. I was mad at myself. I was face to face with the seeming hypocrisy and greed of religion that so many people rebel against. Before Africa, I wouldn't have noticed this box either. I left Notre Dame with a sour taste in my mouth. When I put this movie together, I told myself, I was going to skewer this place. My heart was decidedly not filled with love at that moment.

Fast forward about six months. I was in the throes of editing *Finger of God,* and I had no idea if anyone was ever going to watch this thing or not, but I was still trying to make the most entertaining, uplifting, challenging film I could. God's timing for teaching us never ceases to amaze me, but then again, I don't know why His perfect timing ever surprises me. This is, after all, the God who makes the entire universe run efficiently day after day.

FATHER KNOWS BEST

I was visiting my parents' house in Michigan and had shown my father the first half of this crazy movie I was putting together. He loved what I was doing, and we had quite a few discussions about various parts of the rough cut I had shown him. I was just at the point in editing where I was about to launch into my blistering attack of Notre Dame (this part was my idea, by the way, not God's) where I would pound its greedy rear end into submission. I was going to leave no prisoners. I pictured myself as Jesus storming the temple and driving the money changers out with a whip. Jesus may have been peaceful, but He sure wasn't when it came to religious people. I wasn't going to be peaceful here, I could promise you that. And I told my dad as much.

He paused, weighing his next words carefully. I've had enough conversations with Dad over the years to know when he disagrees with me and is about to say so, and I braced myself for whatever he was about to say. Nothing, absolutely nothing, was going to sway my opinion on this. It was righteous anger, and it was, in my mind, justified. Bring it on, Pop.

"You might want to think about that one, Son," he started. Then he hit me with the line that I was least expecting, and probably the only line that could shake me from my raging intentions. "Remember, it's a lot easier to spew hate and anger than it is to bring love and hope. But love and hope are far more effective. Be careful how you handle this. These are God's people you're dealing with."

You've got to be kidding. How did he pull that one on me? I knew he was right, of course, which infuriated me even more. With a couple of sentences spoken at just the right moment, all my intentions for this section went up in smoke. Shoot, I had even filmed the church with a slamming in mind! How was I supposed to bring hope and love out of footage that was shot with the intention of righteous anger? It was with a heavy heart that I returned to my editing bay upon arriving back in Chicago, realizing that once again I had no idea what I was going to do or how I was going to do it.

So I did the thing that I had done every day up until that point while editing—I prayed for God to give me an idea. How did He want me to portray this place, this injustice, which had to sadden Him at the very least.

The answer came like lightning. It had to be God's idea, because I had something else planned out entirely. I didn't *want* to bring hope to this section, for crying out loud. The thought was simple, yet profound.

"This little, beat up box that no one pays attention to brings Me more glory than all the stained glass in the world."

It was His line, not mine. But as soon as I wrote the words and recorded them to the film, I knew they were right. I knew this was the right approach. I knew I had been wrong. Totally and completely wrong. I had done the very thing that I had denounced for years, and had given in to my own displeasure at a situation by wanting to strike with violence and vehemence.

THEIR ONLY INTERACTION

For many Christians, it seems, the first knee-jerk reaction to something that bothers us is to scream, shout, boycott, or in some way voice our displeasure. I once spoke with a successful producer in Hollywood who is a wonderful Christian man, and he explained to me why so often Christians are portrayed in Hollywood films as bigoted, small minded, angry people. It's because that is the only face of Christianity these directors and producers ever see. Many in Hollywood are not Christians, so they don't know any Christians, which means that the letters they receive or the angry emails or phone calls they receive, or the boycotts they must face are the *only* interaction they have with God's children. It is no wonder, therefore, that we are portrayed as idiots.

We have lost the reputation of love and kindness and peacefulness that God calls for and that was displayed in the early church. A movie or an entertainer may make us angry, but I wonder if boycotting is the best possible way to voice our displeasure. What if we just ignored them? When my son throws a tantrum, if I try to get him to stop, he just screams louder and with more gusto, and does even more outlandish things to show his displeasure. But when I ignore him and walk into another room, it takes maybe 20 seconds before he shuts his trap and realizes that no one is listening to him.

What if we just ignored the stupidity around us? Better yet, what if we combated it with love? What if we prayed for our enemies instead of denouncing them? What if we sincerely wished happiness and blessing on them and their families, and let them know as much through letters and emails stating that, while we disagree with what they are doing or what they have created, God loves them and we love them? How many letters would they need to receive before their own opinions began to change? Before their own hearts would soften to the Father's embrace?

Jesus' declaration to love our enemies and pray for those who hurt us is revolutionary not simply because it defies our basic human response for revenge or justice. It is revolutionary because it goes to the very heart of the Father; it shows us how He responds to our own rebellion, our own attacks against Him, our own stupidity. He pushes our actions aside and moves in for an embrace. We fight Him off, but He absorbs our blows. His eyes never leave ours. His faithfulness to us never wavers despite our best (or worst) efforts.

It is easy to tell people what they are doing wrong, and it feels good to correct people because it elevates our spiritual status—in our own eyes at least. But as my father once told me, at just the right time: it is far more difficult and effective to praise people, to show them what they are doing right, to commend them for it, and to tell and show them how much we love them.

That is God's way of dealing with us, after all.

Chapter 10

LETTING GOD DO IT

Sometimes my job brings me into contact with people and situations that are almost too incredible to believe. I often wonder if I am living in the middle of a science fiction film where the unexplainable becomes normal and the impossible becomes the reality. While filming *Furious Love,* I made a detour to southern India for a couple of days to meet a man many of my friends had been telling me about. It was another one of those, "You've got to meet this guy" things, and even I have to admit that I was overly curious about this one. Apparently, the man I was about to meet, Ravi, hears the audible voice of God. Constantly.

Our first meeting consisted mainly of Ravi telling me stories about his adventures with God, which read like a greatest hits collection of Old Testament prophets and New Testament miracle stories. Since his conversion at age 17, Ravi has heard God speak to him, audibly, outside his head, just as if He were standing right next to him. I wasn't sure I could believe this, but enough people I trust completely were friends with him and vouched for him with such vehemence and extremity, that I was certainly willing to suspend my disbelief until I met him.

It's funny what you expect and what you actually get sometimes when you meet people like Ravi. I was expecting a sage of sorts, an almost mystical man who made me feel like a spiritual toad in relation to his unique gift and privilege. Instead, the man I met was a quiet, unassuming guy, early 30s, who's about as humble as they come; he doesn't speak an ill word about *anyone,* and has such discipline over his spiritual life that it...well, made me feel like a spiritual toad after all.

Having gotten to know Ravi more since then, I began to see why the Father (or as Ravi calls him, Daddy) has trusted him with this gift. My first thought was that this must be the coolest thing ever. After hearing many of Ravi's stories, I'm not so sure anymore. It's still pretty cool, don't get me wrong, but it comes with a heavy responsibility.

I'll go into more of Ravi's story in a later chapter, but for now, I want to tell about the first time I met him and what we did. I had come to meet him while filming *Furious Love,* but I was not allowed to film him—Daddy's orders. Ravi has been asked to allow himself to be filmed a few times over the years, but each time the Lord has answered with a firm no. With me, He told Ravi, "Not yet," which was promising to us both.

One of the things I love about Ravi is how *normal* he is. He freely admitted to me that he was so excited when I contacted him about filming him. His first instinct was, "Absolutely," but he knew he had to ask Daddy first. He was going to be famous. He was going to be in a movie. This was going to be awesome. But then Daddy said no, not yet. You cannot film with Darren for this film. We were both bummed by that (and I have to admit, I questioned God a little on that one. What, don't You trust me?), but we still agreed to meet while I was filming in India so we could get to know one another a little bit. Unbeknownst to me, God had already told Ravi that we were to become great friends, so Ravi already had a leg up on me when I climbed into his car at the airport for the first time.

We had about two days together on our first meeting. Ravi told me story after story of what God had done in his life, and how He had used Ravi for His purposes. The stories I heard were mind-boggling, to say the least. But even after I left him, I still had those nagging doubts, wondering if this guy was for real or if he was just a deranged (yet highly stable) lunatic, or at worst a con man of incredible talent. I mean, how do you verify that someone hears the audible voice of God when they're the only one who can hear it?

I received my answer almost a year later while I sat in my studio in Chicago. In my devotional time that morning, I had asked God a very specific question, but one that I wasn't really expecting an answer to. It was one of those prayers that you kind of throw up to God, and while it means something to you, you realize that you're probably not going to get a specific answer because, well, it's a specific question that would require something akin to an email from God explaining things to you. I was almost sure I wasn't going to be getting one of those, so I threw the prayer up to Him so at least He would know my heart.

Three hours later, my assistant approached me with the phone in her hand and whispered to me, "It's Ravi." With not a little curiosity, I took the phone from her. What the heck? Ravi has *never* called me before. What's this about?

Ravi told me that God had woken him just then (around 3 A.M. in India) and had told him to call me immediately because He wanted to give me a message. Ravi then answered in great detail the very question I had asked the Lord that morning. It wasn't an email from God, it was a personal phone call! What do you do with something like that? Well, for starters, I had to admit that yes, I think Ravi might just be the real deal.

RAVI'S INDIA

I was standing in a village in southern India. Narrow lanes of wood and brick houses jutted out from the center of the village in different directions, and the place looked like a ghost town. Everyone had gathered at the little meeting center in the middle of the village (basically an open structure with a roof). Everyone, that is, except for the men.

Roughly 50 people sat on the floor in front of me. All of them women and children. The Lord had told Ravi to come to this village today and to bring this team with him. I was tagging along with a group of around 12 Americans and Europeans who had come on an evangelistic trip put on by Shara Pradhan, Heidi Baker's former Personal Assistant. Ravi took me aside and explained what was going on. He knew, obviously, because he had seen this before.

The Lord had brought him to this village, on this particular day, just as he had done with nearly 300 other villages over the years. Sometimes, if Ravi knows where the place is, the Lord will simply tell him the name of the place. Other times, He will give him turn-by-turn directions as he drives. Take a left here. Right here. Hang a left there. Soon he'll find himself smack in the middle of a village he never knew existed. And the adventure begins.

Today, though, we were in a village God had pointed out to Ravi and he had his marching orders. He was to have a member of the team speak to the women and children, present the Gospel, and Ravi would interpret. For that particular day, the Lord chose a soft-spoken girl in her early 20s who had never preached publicly before and was about as terrified as I would have been had Ravi asked me to do such a thing. She managed through it the best she could (he didn't warn her ahead of time—God's orders), and the people listened with rapt attention. Heads would train on the young woman, then turn to Ravi when she had finished speaking, as if they were watching a tennis match.

Then Ravi asked how many people would like to accept Jesus as their Savior. All hands went up. Ravi spoke to them with a seriousness that belied his easygoing nature, and I made a mental note to ask him what he was telling them at that moment. They looked back at him solemnly, and nodded their heads in agreement. Huh. Interesting.

Ravi then had the entire team roam among the people and pray for them individually, which we heartily did. Afterward, we went to the little school in the village and had lunch with the kids. Ravi and I sat, and I finally got to ask my questions.

"So, where are all the men?"

"They are hiding."

"From what?"

"From us," he replied, quite matter-of-fact. "They know who we are and why we are here. They want nothing to do with us. The women and children, though, were curious."

I remembered him speaking to the people so seriously and asked him what that was about.

BEATINGS AHEAD

"I was telling them that they will most certainly be beaten by their husbands and fathers for what they have done today. I told them that if they can keep their faith for two weeks, despite this persecution, they will win over their husbands. They too will believe."

I stared at him in disbelief.

"What if that doesn't happen?" I'm certain my voice betrayed my judgment that this was a fairly insane statement to make to people heading into beatings.

"It always happens. I have gone to 267 villages. This is village 268. It is always the same. Two weeks, and the men realize that the women and children are serious. They either give up, or grow curious."

At that point, another thought hit me.

"Ravi, what's to keep these people from just adding Jesus to their pantheon of gods?"

The Hindu religion, after all, has, like, 300 million gods.

"Oh, that's exactly what they'll do."

I almost spit out my food. What the heck were we doing here if Jesus was just going to join all their other gods on the shelf? Ravi obviously sensed my concern.

"You forget, Darren, that my Daddy is a jealous God. He doesn't want to be lumped together with a bunch of false gods. So I let Him take care of it. Here is what will happen.

They will begin praying to this new God, just as they do all the others. What will be different, though, is they will begin to see that the God of the Bible actually answers their prayers when they pray to Him. Eventually, they will realize that the God of the Bible is the *only* God who answers their prayers, and they will approach me and tell me they want to get rid of all of their idols. That is when we will have a big bonfire in the village and burn all of their other, past gods."

I was dumbfounded. I'd never heard of a Christian doing this before. Letting God do the work of conviction. I grew up in an environment, in a worldview, that implied that it was our job as Christians to show people what they were doing wrong, and to teach them the ways good Christians are supposed to act. But this encounter with Ravi only confirmed what I was beginning to sense from the various testimonies I had heard over the years from people who came out of places of extreme sin or darkness.

Almost every person related to me that it was God, not a preacher, who showed them what they were doing was wrong. It no longer felt right. It no longer felt good. Their eyes were opened to their own failures by the Holy Spirit living and moving inside of them. This was a radical shift, and it provided me with a new wrinkle for the film I was making. Pursue God, and let *Him* do the rest. Pursue a relationship with Christ, and let God change you.

A NEW TRUTH

I was no longer dealing with a God of principles or 12-step programs. I was dealing with a God who, if we let Him, would invade our very lives and clean out the junk. He is willing to meet us on our own terms, in our present situations. We don't need to prepare ourselves for His presence anymore. We don't need to "get ourselves right" before He will be willing to meet with us.

If one of my children went off the deep end and fell into a life of radical sin, and did everything they possibly could to harm themselves, I would never, ever force them to clean themselves up first if they called me for help. I would find them wherever they were, and if I had to sit in sewage to get to them, I would do it without blinking.

How much more is God willing to meet us in our putrid state?

This truth was played out again when, a few months later, I was again filming for *Furious Love,* but this time found myself smack in the middle of a New Age festival in Mount Shasta, California. It was a minor miracle that they let us film there, but since I was making a movie about love, and the theme for the festival that year was "unconditional love," I think they would have felt a little silly had they told me no.

We were given our limitations when we arrived: no calling anyone "New Age wackos," no telling anyone they were going to hell, no selling Christian propaganda, stuff like that. I had brought a team of about ten people with me who were not interested in doing anything of the sort; they just wanted the opportunity to pray for people, no strings attached. If God wanted to move, then we were making ourselves available for Him to do so. But this was His show, not ours.

The festival was a little different from what I had imagined. Events like these usually are, so I had to readjust my expectations as soon as we arrived. Instead of being outside, like I thought, we were shoved into a corner of a gymnasium where people were selling their products. We set up our cameras, put people in prayer teams, and started asking whoever might be interested if they'd like some prayer.

We caused quite a stir. The people who came to us for prayer loved us. They all went away feeling loved, and some had some profound experiences with the Lord. Others in the room, though, weren't so happy. Apparently we were screwing up their "vibe," and more than one person went to the folks in charge and told them to kick us out—that we were Christians, and we weren't welcome there.

One of my team members overheard one of these conversations and was intrigued that the person in charge answered one of the protestors by telling him that he had tried twice to kick us out, but that he "just couldn't do it." When the protestor asked him what he meant, why he couldn't do it, the guy answered that he didn't know. He had walked up to me twice, but before he could say anything, he just stopped and stood there and stared at me. It was like he couldn't move or talk. He was confused by it all, and since we technically weren't hurting anybody, there wasn't a whole lot more he could do. The protestor stormed off in a huff.

One woman I filmed had an amazing story to tell. I filmed her as my friend Chris Overstreet and my sister Danielle prayed for her. I could tell right away that she was having a major experience of some kind. Tears streamed down her face, and her smile was radiant. Afterward, she told us what had happened to her only a week ago.

CHANNELING THE GREAT I AM

She was heading out to her mailbox when she heard a voice—an audible voice—speak to her. She stopped and demanded: "Whoever you are, show yourself." A Man instantly appeared in front of her, standing next to her mailbox, and He was bathed in light. He introduced Himself to her as Jesus. He told her that He wanted her to go to this particular event in Mount Shasta the following week and that He would meet her there. He then disappeared.

When she approached Chris and Danielle, they asked her if she knew Jesus. "Oh yes," she replied, "I'm channeling the great I Am right now."

I remember the moment she said those words to me. My insides felt a little lurch, and part of me wanted to correct her and explain to her that "channeling" stuff was New Agey, and that she wasn't supposed to be doing that anymore. She was supposed to go to church, and say this one particular prayer, and burn all her New Age books in the process. But then I thought of Ravi and those women in India, and how Ravi put his trust in God's jealousy for His Bride, and I relaxed a little. Years ago, this lady would have freaked me out. The language she used was so thick with New Age lingo that I wondered if I needed to take a spiritual bath afterward, but she was simply using the only language she understood. She had just been marked by my Lord, and He wasn't going to let her get away from Him without a fight.

I realize that many would argue that it is indeed our job to show people the error of their ways, and I would agree up to a point. Ravi's whole goal is to get these people to burn their idols, but he also realizes that if it is *he* who forces them to do it, the change will not be as great or as secure as it will be when *God* is the One who compels them. The woman at Mount Shasta told us there was a church she attended off and on, and that she was now interested in going there more. Isn't that what God intended for her? It took everything within me to keep my mouth shut and just enjoy this moment of pure love the woman was experiencing. She was so grateful to us, so bowled over by what had happened to her within the last week, she didn't quite know how to even put it in words.

ONLY GOD KNOWS

Was this woman a Christian now? I have no idea. Only God knows that, but I have to believe that just as God will eventually gain total control of the hearts of Ravi's Hindu women and children, so will He jealously go after this woman's heart until she either succumbs to His love completely, or stops breathing. For one week of her life at least, she experienced the one, true God. It is only a matter of time, I have to believe, before He loves her into His arms alone.

The church is known less for its love and more for its issues of control. The church service has to end at a particular time. We can only sing the songs that are scheduled for today. The order of the service must follow a pre-patterned sequence. If you are going to call yourself a Christian, then you better not have any problems.

But what would the church look like if we let go, even a little, of our own control over how church is done? What would happen if our primary focus was to invite the presence of the Most High into our midst? What would church look like if we didn't just focus on *experiencing* Him, but in doing on a day-to-day basis what He has commanded us to do? Love unconditionally. Love each other. Love the lost. Love ourselves. Love God with abandon.

It took me having to travel around the world before I could finally realize that God can indeed do better work in peoples' hearts than I can. It is His job to convict, not ours. When we do it, shame and guilt are the consequences. When God does it, the result is change.

Chapter 11

GOD, YOU'VE GOT TO BE KIDDING ME

I find it one of the great ironies of irony that, as a result of *Finger of God,* I have become something of an "expert" on the miraculous to some people. I of course am anything but an expert, but it is true that I have seen a lot—enough to pull me out of the unbelieving camp and into the cautious, "anything is possible with God" crew. But the mere fact that people often search me out for my opinions on incredibly difficult questions about the miraculous God we serve never ceases to amaze me. I mean, I was about as skeptical as a person can get about this stuff before I started making *Finger.* And now people are coming to me to figure out why God heals some and doesn't heal others? Are they sure they're talking to the right person?

That being said, I've never been shy about having an opinion, especially once I have seen and experienced both sides of the debate. In my experience, the main hurdle many people must overcome before they will fully put their trust in a God who loves them enough that He might possibly heal them through miraculous means is to come to an understanding that He might *not* heal them. The question, then, is what do you think of *that* God? Everyone loves a God who has mercy on them and heals them when they probably don't deserve it. But what about a God who doesn't heal someone who, maybe, does deserve it? Like a child? That is the moment when the rubber meets the road and your faith is officially put to the test.

When I was in the middle of filming *Finger of God* and my faith in a miraculous God was constantly being reinforced, a young couple who were friends with my wife and me and were nearing the end of their first pregnancy were given the horrendous news that their baby had died inside the womb. It was about as devastating as things can get, and our church rallied around them in prayer and support. A small pocket of us even went so far as to pray for a full-blown resurrection within the womb. The baby was delivered, and he was still lifeless. It was a blow to this young couple, good friends of ours, that, to this day, has shaken their faith and trust in a God who they thought loved them and would watch out for them.

To be honest, it's hard to blame them.

FAITH TESTED

One of my most bitter defeats came when we had just begun filming *Furious Love.* We were at a crusade in Tanzania with Jeff Jansen and a big team that had gathered to help preach and pray for people. At this point, we had just begun filming, and I didn't quite have a handle on what exactly God was going to be leading us to film—what story He wanted us to tell. Part of me thought that maybe we would be making *Finger of God 2,* with a little more emphasis on spiritual warfare than miracles, but I wasn't sure. Typically, when you're unsure as an artist, you will fall back on old patterns that worked in the past, and in Tanzania, this was no exception. I paid much more attention to miracles that were or might be happening around me than I did to anything else.

During the evening a little later in the week, we encountered a truly heart-wrenching scene. We were told that a father had just arrived with his young daughter, and he was begging the team to come and pray for his little girl. She had lockjaw and could not open her mouth more than an inch. She couldn't speak. She had to eat using a straw. We went off to the side and surrounded this father and daughter and began praying. While the prayers intensified, I asked around to try and understand the situation more. Apparently this father had heard that there were people in Arusha who were praying for people and healing them. At great cost, he and his daughter had just traveled over ten hours to get her to us.

I looked at this little girl, who was around the same age as my own daughter, saw her straining to open her mouth wide, saw the tears streaming down her precious cheeks as she slowly began to realize that she wasn't going to be healed. I watched her father hold her close, praying just as fervently, asking, begging, groveling to God to have mercy on his child. Heal her. Please. We prayed with authority. We prayed with complete faith. We begged. We pleaded.

I remember thinking when we started that surely if there was a time God would heal someone, this was it. A desperate father does all he can, in faith, to get his daughter in front of other believers who believed in the healing power of Christ, and had seen many healings themselves. This was a poor family, and it had cost the father of this girl much to get her here. God loves the poor. God loves the faithful. God loves the children. This is it, I remember praying as I filmed. God, this is Your time to show this family how much You love them. Show the world how great You are.

But nothing happened.

The girl wasn't healed.

We left the girl and her father and headed back to our hotel. They walked back to their car no better than before we began. It was one of the most bitter defeats I've ever had.

I sat silent in the bus on the way back to the hotel. Inside I was seething. God, how could You? How could You just sit there and watch this little girl and do nothing? It would take nothing from You, nothing to simply command her to be healed! How can You call Yourself merciful when You allow stuff like this to continue?

Through the years, I have encountered many people with stories similar to that little girl with lockjaw. The person may change—a son, a sister, a parent, a friend—but the result is always the same. They aren't healed. They continue a life of pain. They die. And the result is usually the same as well. The people who believed find it much, much harder to believe that God is as loving as He claims. Some stop believing altogether.

We know in our heads that God is love, but sometimes when He refuses to lift His hand to heal someone who desperately needs it, things get difficult. Faith gets tested. Many turn away because they refuse to believe in a God who could be so cold as to allow this suffering when He can just as easily relieve it with a simple command.

DEFENDER OF THE MIRACULOUS

And this is the question I am faced with most often in my newfound, wholly ironic role as defender of the miraculous. Why does God heal some people and not others? I have heard lots of opinions on the matter, but very few that I find appealing or logical. In fact, I reject the two biggest excuses I most often hear from the Charismatic crowd I often run with.

The first is that the person praying didn't have enough faith. I know this can't be true, simply because I saw with my own two eyes while filming *Furious Love* that someone with *no faith* (me) could pray for someone else and see them healed (see Chapter 5). Obviously, faith will often play a role, but to turn it into a general rule is an attempt to turn God's healing nature into a formula, and since God is creativity personified, He will never be placed within a formula.

The second argument I often hear is that the person receiving prayer didn't have enough faith. This seems bogus on so many levels. In essence, you are blaming the person receiving prayer for not receiving what they are asking for. Even when Jesus encountered this in someone, He didn't shy away from healing them. In Mark 9, a father approaches Jesus with his son who is possessed by a demon and asks Jesus if He can help his son. Jesus replies, "If you can? Everything is possible for him who believes." The boy's father responds with a desperate, *"I believe! Help my unbelief!"* At this point, he'll say whatever he needs to say to help his son. Jesus then saw the crowds running and healed the boy.

So the question begs to be answered, was it the father claiming that he believed (followed quickly by an admission that he didn't believe a whole lot, but could sure use some help right now) that provided the magic words Jesus needed to heal his son? It is important to note, I think, that just a few verses prior to this encounter, Jesus' disciples had tried unsuccessfully to drive out the demon. It's no wonder that the boy's father was a tad conflicted when asked if he believed Jesus could do this, if His own disciples couldn't do it. Jesus, of course, healed the boy, and was later questioned by His disciples as to why they weren't able to drive out the demon themselves. Jesus replies that "this kind can only come out by prayer." If Jesus hadn't been there, the boy wouldn't have been healed. And no one present would have known or understood why. They just would have figured that God was silent when He was really needed.

The problem with the two arguments given here lies in the fact that in both instances, it's *our* responsibility to bring about a positive result. If God doesn't heal, well, then it must be our fault. Either the person who is praying or the person receiving the prayer didn't have enough faith.

But this reasoning, in effect, turns us into magicians, and our magic will only work if we can just clear our minds and our hearts enough. Look, I am not going to discount the role we may play when we pray for someone, but I would argue that the mere act of stepping out in faith, with the very real possibility of failure, is about the extent that we will play in whether or not someone is healed. God has healed through some pretty bad dudes over the years, and He has healed more than a few atheists. So to pin the blame on individuals is, I think, giving ourselves a little too much credit. In the end, *only God heals,* and it's always on His terms.

But what about those hard moments when, say, children are involved, or something unjust has happened to someone and we're now simply asking for justice or deserved mercy? If it truly is God calling the shots, then aren't we right back where we started from? Aren't we back to wondering how a loving God could be so...unloving?

SPIRITUAL FORCES OF EVIL

This was a question I wrestled with for a long time, until I met a man by the name of Greg Boyd. I was in the middle of filming *Furious Love,* and a pastor friend of mine told me that if I was making a film about good and evil, then I had to get my hands on some books written by Greg. *God at War* and *Satan and the Problem of Evil* transformed my theology, and answered a bunch of questions in the process. They also put Greg Boyd smack in the middle of *Furious Love.*

His books are heavy reading, but the point is simple. We are in a war. This war is not against flesh and blood, *"but against the rulers, against the authorities, against the cosmic powers over this present darkness, against the spiritual forces of evil in the heavenly places"* (Eph. 6:12). And as with all wars, there is going to be catastrophe, heartache, and collateral damage, and good people are going to get hurt. We tend to believe that since God has the ability to control everything, He is therefore controlling everything. But He has made it abundantly clear throughout the Scriptures that He is fully invested in free will, both for us and for the heavenly realms.

In Daniel 10:12-14, there is a curious encounter between Daniel and the angel Gabriel. Three weeks prior, Daniel had prayed for assistance from the Lord, and Gabriel was dispatched immediately to tend to him. But, in the words of Gabriel, he was "delayed" by the prince of the Persian kingdom (a demonic principality) and only got through to Daniel because God sent the archangel Michael, one of the big dogs, to free things up for Gabriel to finally get to Daniel.

In his books, Greg Boyd goes to great lengths to flesh out the meaning of this as well as other passages throughout the Bible that clearly show that God is at war with satan and his demons. While this may seem obvious (I was taught this as a kid, for goodness sake), its implications appear to have been overlooked by just about every Christian I know. If you are at war with someone, that someone will typically go after the very targets that are most precious to you.

And what is most precious to God? His Word makes the answer to this question clear. Us—His children. So from the very beginning of it all, satan has focused almost exclusively on terrorizing us. Jesus said in John 10:10 that the enemy, the thief, comes only to steal and kill and destroy. That is his job, wholly and completely. Ruin everything that is good and beautiful to God.

Because God has set up certain rules for His world (free will being perhaps the biggest), He must in turn fight His battles within those rules. While we may be uncertain about much, we can rely on one foundational truth. Just as the enemy comes to take life (both literally and figuratively), Jesus has come to bring us life, and that we may live life to the fullest. He comes to bless us, never to harm us.

For most of my life I had a serious problem with God. How could He allow so many bad things to happen to people and not do anything about it? How could a loving God turn His back on a woman with a dead baby in her belly who is crying out for Him to bring the child back to life? How could

He ignore the desperation of a father for his young girl who cannot even open her mouth? Why is He doing this to us?

WHY?

Jesus' disciples asked the same question of Jesus in John 9:2 when they inquired who had sinned, the man or his parents. Who caused this man before them to be blind? It was obviously something we had done. Jesus, of course, replied that neither had caused this. This man's blindness wasn't God's retribution, as the disciples thought. It simply provided another opportunity for God to show His glory.

When bad things happen to us, our first, natural instinct is often to turn on God and ask Him why He did this to us. But we forget the fact that we are in a war, and that God is not the enemy. Our enemy is real, highly motivated, and hates us with a passion precisely because God loves us so much. It is him who brings sickness. It is him who brings pain. It is him who brings death. He is the one we should be fighting, not God. We are fighting against agents of evil who have wills of their own, who try, and often succeed, to thwart God's plans for us (see Dan. 10).

In truth, we have no idea why, when we pray for someone, they do or do not get healed. The only person who truly knows that answer is God, and it is not His duty to explain every decision He makes to us. We cannot see into the spiritual realm. We cannot see into the heart of man. We cannot know all the subtleties and intricacies of the entire human experience, of generational sin, or of opened spiritual doors, or of what the demonic realm has a right over in our lives at that moment.

But God *does* have access to all of that knowledge. And His judgments are always right, always fair, and always good, even when, to us, they may seem wrong.

We live in a world where bad things happen to good people all the time. When we became Christians, God did not promise us a life of ease and of total protection from the enemy. In fact, He promised us the exact opposite. They will hate us; they will persecute us. But even in our sorrow, even in our despair, even in our trials, His love for us will never fade. He will never leave us or forsake us (see Deut. 31:6; Heb. 13:5).

Why does God allow some to be healed and some to remain sick? I have no idea. When Jesus healed the man at the pool of Bethesda in John 5, we tend to forget that the place was swarming with disabled and hurting people, yet Jesus chose to heal only one of them. Does this make Jesus' compassion any less potent? Not for that one, I can assure you.

And Scripture is loaded with evidence pointing us to the knowledge that even if our prayers may not be answered the way we want them to be, His compassion and love for us will never fade. There are a million reasons why our prayers may not lead to healing, but it is my contention that those reasons are God's reasons. We never know if a person's time has come for a healing touch from God, so we are commanded to go and do as Jesus did, which is to preach the Gospel, heal the sick, raise the dead, cleanse the lepers, and drive out demons.

OBEDIENCE IS NONNEGOTIABLE

Our job is to be obedient and allow God to move if He deems the time is right. The rest is up to Him. It is always

His desire to heal, but sometimes the junk of this world, of our past, of the invisible realm—the rules set down at the foundation of the world—keep His will from happening.

I have made mention of my friend in India, Ravi, who hears the audible voice of the Lord every day. I asked him once if he ever ignores the voice when it asks him to do something. He laughed and said yes, he has ignored it. I then asked what happens when he does that, and he gave a shy grin and answered, "Very bad things."

He told me a story once about how he was preaching in a village and a man in the crowd was cursing him and, at one point, punched him while he was sharing the Gospel. Weeks later, he saw the man again, and his arm was bandaged. God spoke to Ravi and told him to go pray for that man; God wanted to heal him. Ravi replied that he would do no such thing. "That hand struck me. I will not pray for it to be healed." The Lord replied evenly, yet firmly. "I said, I want to heal him. Now go pray for him." Ravi flatly refused. The man did not receive healing (and one could assume, salvation) because the person God had chosen to be His hands and feet in this situation said no.

The next day Ravi was rushed to the hospital where he spent the next few weeks deathly ill. To whom much is given, of him much is expected (see Luke 12:48), and Ravi has been given much indeed with this gift from God. He had a clear, obvious task set before him, and he chose to allow his own prejudices to get the better of him. How often do we hear not an audible voice, but perhaps that still, small voice, like a whisper, asking us to step out and pray for someone? It is a request that may cause us embarrassment and will at the very least make us uncomfortable. It may make us late. It may announce that we are Christians to people who we would prefer not know.

But what if we said yes? And what if we prayed and nothing happened? One, God would be happy with us, because we had passed His test and shown Him that we love Him more than we love our own ego. But what might happen to that person? A stranger approaches and has the nerve, the sheer gall to ask us if we could pray for them. Nothing happens, and they may be disappointed, but might they also feel loved? Might they feel like there are still decent and caring people in the world? Might the reputation of Christians, and in turn, the reputation of Christ, benefit? Just as there are a million reasons why God may not heal someone, so there are a million other reasons why we are to simply be obedient and step out in faith and love to pray for the hurting world around us.

Lest I be misunderstood, I do not discount the importance of faith aiding in the release of the miraculous love of God. Faith is absolutely essential. I may not have believed that God was going to heal that guy in Africa when I prayed for him, but I certainly believed that God *does* heal. I have seen firsthand the power of testimony to usher in a wave of similar healings in a church or even a living room. I have also seen the crippling effects of someone who simply cannot get past their own intellectual objections to the whole exercise of praying for healing.

Extreme faith can bring healing, just as doubt can prevent it. It's not that I reject teachings on these finer points of the equation, I simply think that to reduce God and how He chooses to release His power upon us to a formula that can be found in a workbook is entirely missing the point. He is God. I am His child. I am here to do His will. His will is to bring freedom to a dying world, and often that freedom will be a freedom from physical suffering as well. In order to bring that freedom, I am asked to pray for others. If God moves at the time I pray, then the person will most likely find their freedom. But if there are things, either in the natural or spiritual realms, that can get in the way of God's will moving forward upon this person, then we're probably going to have a bit of trouble.

It's not complicated, but it's not easy either.

We are told to weep for those who weep. Rejoice with those who rejoice. In all things praise God. In all things care for others. In all things, love and know that you are loved.

The rest is just life in the midst of a war.

Chapter 12

TRUST IS A LOT HARDER THAN IT LOOKS

So let's talk about Ravi, shall we? I realize that at this point, you're probably eager to know more about this guy, so I figure it's about time to fill you in on his story and introduce him to you properly. He will be featured in the next film of the *Finger of God/Furious Love* series (entitled, *Father of Lights*) because, well, because God said so.

I've never met anyone remotely like Ravi. Sure, I've met scores of people who claim they speak to God on a regular basis, that He tells them what to do, that He has even visited them on occasion, but Ravi is wholly unique due to the fact that he hears the audible voice of God speaking directly to him every day.

Obviously, when I first heard about him, I knew immediately that I had to meet him, and then, even more importantly, I had to film him! I tried, trust me. I had friends ask him. I asked him through email. I asked him personally. Each time, he came back with the same answer. "No. Sorry. Daddy says no." It's no stretch to say that when I realized I wouldn't be allowed to film him, I was bummed beyond belief. When I flew to Southern India to meet him while filming *Furious Love,* I considered it a chance to meet an extraordinary man, but my dreams of filming with him were gone.

NOT YET

We became friends almost immediately. We're nearly the same age, we have similar personalities, and, most importantly to me, the guy wasn't nuts. This was the possibility that worried me most before I met him. I mean, I had never met anyone before who could talk to God audibly all the time, and I was suspending my disbelief until I met him. I secretly wondered if this guy was just very astute at observing people and simply told them what they wanted to hear. At least, that's what I was bracing myself for.

When I finally met him, though, I was disarmed by his easygoing nature, his incredible humility, and his very real, very human condition. He admitted to me early on that when he first heard I wanted to film with him, he was elated, and his immediate response was *yes!* He admitted that he was excited to become famous, to be in a movie. But then "the Voice" spoke to him. He was in the bathroom, and the Lord said quite clearly, "You haven't asked Me yet...."

He knew what was coming. But he asked anyway. "Daddy, can I do it?"

"Not yet," was the answer.

He argued with God. He asked God why he couldn't. In fact, he asked God at least three times, yet each time he received the same answer. "Not yet." No matter what, Ravi was not going to be in *Furious Love.*

But I wanted to meet him anyway, so while I was filming in India, I made a special trip to his home to meet him, just in case Daddy ever said we could film in the future. That's when Ravi first told me that the Lord hadn't said no entirely, just not yet. Big difference. It meant he would *probably* let us film together in the future. So we discussed what we might film together.

"How about this," he said. "Why don't you just come out here and I'll ask Daddy what we should do. Then He'll tell us where to go and what to do, and we'll do it. And you can film it."

Sounded great to me! It's what I was secretly hoping for but was still too afraid at that point to ask. I mean, how do you treat someone with that kind of a gift? I wasn't sure yet if it was the kind of thing you casually talk about, or, you know, if it was too sacred to bring up. As our friendship has grown, so has my ability to talk to him about his gift and how he deals with it. He has made no secret that it is not easy. When you hear from the Lord so clearly, you have little choice but to obey. It's not like he can claim ignorance or anything. Plus, and this is what I didn't realize until I got to know him better, the Lord typically does not tell him *why* he is supposed to do a specific thing, simply that he is to *do it.*

AS A FRIEND

So quite often Ravi will find himself having to do something that is entirely out of his comfort zone, or very strange, and he will never see the reason he was told to do such a thing. It is a tough life, but one that is built on the trust that God loves him as His son, and he is not simply a hired hand to do His bidding. In fact, as Ravi described it to me, often the Lord tells him way more about someone than Ravi is allowed to share. He told me once that if he were God, he would just tell the person to say this and this and that, and don't worry about anything else. But God speaks to him as a friend, as if He's *excited* about how He is going to bless or use someone.

Ravi gets to share in that excitement with the Lord, but it also carries a heavy price. Imagine having such wonderful foreknowledge of what the Lord has planned for your best friends, but you are not allowed to mention any of it to them. He gave me a glimpse of what it was like when he shared a few things with me about some mutual friends of ours. I'm not allowed to say anything to them (and I fully understand why—it could seriously mess with your head if you know too much about your future), and it totally stinks that I can't say anything! It's like having an amazing Christmas gift for someone, but you don't know when they'll be receiving it, and you can't say you know what they're getting.

I think of my own spiritual journey, and I realize that the biggest hurdle I had to overcome was my willingness and ability to trust God. I needed to trust that He was looking out for my best interests, and that He wasn't just intent on using me for whatever He wanted me for, regardless of what I wanted or cared about. God was, for most of my life, very impersonal. I mean, He was *God*. He was enormous, every-where, dealt with everyone, was incredibly busy, and, accord-ing to the way church had portrayed Him, He was pretty darn serious.

I tend to fall a little more into the "laid back" category, so the idea of having a relationship with a serious, anal, type A God was more than a little daunting, and felt more formal than passionate.

But then I began to experience God more, and I watched Him move on, in, and through people all over the world. I began to get a clearer picture of His personality, and I began to read the Bible through new eyes. God isn't a stern, judg-mental, overly serious control freak. He's not just using all of us as puppets for His cosmic struggle with the devil. He honestly longs for a love relationship with us. He wants to be our Father and exhibits only the good, amazing traits of a loving, devoted father in the process. He's not abusive. He's not harsh. He's not overbearing. He is love.

And if we truly believe that God the Father is love, then we must therefore believe that He, as a Father, is patient, kind, and gentle. He doesn't envy, He isn't proud, He's not rude, He's not self-seeking, He's not easily angered, He keeps no record of wrongs. He doesn't delight in evil, but rejoices with the truth. He always protects, always trusts, always hopes, always perseveres. He never fails.

That God looks a lot different from the God I grew up with. That's a God I can walk arm in arm with, and one I can *trust* with everything I do and with all that I am. He sees the entire picture, while I see a mere sliver. He wants what is best for me; in the same way, He wants me to give myself over to His will completely.

Once I reconciled those two seemingly clashing ideologies and resolved myself to the fact that His will would always take my heart into account, then I could finally let go and offer myself up to Him. So I did just that on a cold, December night in 2005, and the next thing that entered my mind was the beginning of *Finger of God*. My life and my happiness would never be the same again.

SUICIDE JUMP

It is easy to wax theological about these things, and it is quite another to put them into practice when what God is asking us seems like...well...suicide. In Ravi's case, it was more literal than figurative.

He told me a story he lovingly refers to as "the train story." This will give you an idea of what it might be like for you if God decided to bestow this unique gift of hearing His audible voice on a regular basis. Be careful what you wish for....

Ravi was traveling to a conference in India put on by some American evangelists. He was going to hear the teaching, yes, but he was mostly going for the food. At this point in his life, Ravi had very little money, and the prospect of getting some good eats while hearing the Word of God preached was simply too much to pass up. So he donned his best white shirt, complete with intricate embroidery across the breast (to hear him tell it, this was the greatest shirt ever made. In reality, it was the only nice shirt he owned!), hopped on a train, and cracked open his Bible to read during the journey.

About halfway through the train ride, he heard that familiar voice of Daddy.

"Jump off the train."

His first instinct was to rebuke that evil spirit in Jesus' name. And that's just what he did. But the voice kept speaking, and it was a voice he knew well.

"Jump off the train. I want you to jump off the train."

Ravi began to have an argument with God. The train was going fast, and as he looked out the window, he resolved that there was no way he was going to do what Daddy was asking this time. This wasn't a request, it was suicide.

Yet the voice persisted. "Jump. Jump. Jump…"

He tried to ask God why He wanted him to jump off the train.

"Just jump."

He tried to show God what He obviously wasn't realizing. Ravi may not die in the jump, but he would certainly be grievously injured. How could God be glorified if that happened?

"Just jump."

"Ask somebody else to jump."

"Jump."

For 20 minutes Ravi argued with God. He tried to bargain with God. Not once did the Lord ever tell him why He was asking Ravi to do this. He just expected obedience based on trust from His friend.

Reluctantly, Ravi got up from his seat, Bible in tow, and went out of the train car onto the landing linking the two cars together. The Indian countryside whizzed by him, and the roar of the wheels on the track was deafening. Was the train speeding up? God, I'm going to die if I do this.

"Just jump."

He wasn't going to do it. He couldn't do it. He was frozen to the spot. What is the point of doing this, he kept asking himself. He still wondered if it was the devil trying to trick him, but it couldn't be; he knew that voice too well. He had heard it since he became a Christian at age 17.

Suddenly, as if Jesus Himself were standing directly behind him, the voice screamed in his ear, "Jump now!" and he felt two hands push him, hard, off the train.

I never asked Ravi what he was thinking as he flew through the air at that moment. My guess is, before he hit the ground, the lone thought was something along the lines of, *Who the heck just pushed me?!* That thought would have been swallowed up immediately by the impact his body made when it hit the...mud?

Ravi didn't realize it when he was standing on the train, but at the exact moment he jumped, the train was passing a construction site. There had been a lot of rain lately, and along the edge of this construction area a giant pool of mud and water had collected near the bottom of the train tracks. Ravi jumped (or was pushed, depending on how you look at it) at the exact moment this pool of mud came into view. He landed in the soft mud and, as he puts it, was "baptized in mud." This wasn't a high church sprinkling on the head, this was full-on, Bible-belt submersion. He came up gasping for air and watched as the last car of the train snarled away from him. He then looked down and remembered what shirt he was wearing. There was no washing machine in the world that would get out this stain.

"Great. Thanks a lot, God, look what you did to my shirt!" I believe that was his first reaction. It wasn't until he was slowly pulling himself out of the mud pit that he noticed...the other guy, 30 feet away, who was doing the same thing.

They regarded each other carefully, until Ravi was the first to voice what they were obviously both thinking.

"Hey, did you just jump off that train?"

"Yes," the man replied.

"Why did you do that?"

"I was trying to kill myself," was his simple reply. "Why did you jump?"

"Don't ask," was all Ravi said. It was bad enough that God had ruined his shirt, he wasn't about to make himself look like a complete idiot.

INSTRUMENT OF HOPE

As they both exited the mud pit, Ravi knew why the Lord had pushed him off the train at that precise moment. It was for this guy. God knew this guy was in such a bad place that he was going to try to kill himself, and since Ravi was on the train, He would be God's instrument of hope for this man.

The only problem was, Ravi wasn't entirely excited with God at the moment. He definitely wasn't going to get to the conference in time to get some good food, and his best shirt had just been completely destroyed. Plus, come on, the Lord had just pushed him off a moving train!

Realizing that he would either do this thing or the whole ordeal would be for nothing, he approached the man and began telling him about Jesus. Of course, as Ravi puts it, he preached to the man "very angrily." This wasn't what he wanted to be doing at the moment, but he did it because he knew he was supposed to. So he presented the Gospel of love while malice overtook his heart, but the man heard every word and eagerly asked to accept Jesus as his Savior.

This didn't really affect Ravi the way the Lord maybe hoped it would, because he was still furious. His job now officially done, he then saw a nearby pond where they both might be able to rinse some of this mud off. As they walked over to it, Ravi grudgingly asked the man another question.

"Hey, do you want to be baptized?"

"What is 'baptized'?" was the man's reply.

"Don't worry about it, just come with me."

Ravi baptized him, thus washing the man's sins away along with the mud. They shook hands and parted ways. Ravi called some friends who lived nearby and they picked him up, gave him clothes to borrow, and he arrived at the conference three hours late.

The other man had walked off to begin his new life.

Months later, Ravi was attending yet another conference. He felt a tap on his shoulder and turned to see a man smiling at him.

"Can I help you?" he asked.

"Pastor, do you not remember me? I was the one who jumped off the train with you awhile back."

"Oh yes, yes," Ravi replied, "how could I forget!"

"I wanted to thank you for introducing me to Jesus, and I wanted you to know that I went back to my village that very day and began preaching about Him to my friends and family. Today I am the pastor of my village, and it is all because you jumped off that train with me at the same time! Is God amazing or what?"

Ravi hugged the man and wished him well. He then went to a quiet place and cried his eyes out. He repented for not trusting his Father, for yelling at Him, for preaching His message of love out of anger. And he promised the Lord that if He ever asks him to jump off a train again, he will do it with gusto.

NOT ABOUT RAVI

Ravi is just a man, and he will be the first to admit it. Even after God spoke to him one morning, entirely out of the blue, and told him that he could now film with me (He actually said my name, which I think is about the coolest, most humbling thing ever), the Lord then added that I would have to blur Ravi's face. This was not to be about Ravi. This was to be about what a mighty God can do through a simple, ordinary man like Ravi. He humbly accepted this, and I have to admit, I wasn't surprised. It sounded like something God would do.

Ravi told me he has met Jesus in the flesh five times in his life. The first time occurred when the Lord asked him to commit to a 40-day fast (water only). Ravi mentioned that fasting and Ravi do not go well together, so this was a major request from the Lord. He said he would do it under two conditions: 1) that he would be allowed to meet the voice that speaks to him in person; and 2) that the Lord would show him who his wife would be.

I AM THE ONE

With a few days left in his fast, Ravi was sitting in his room praying when a brilliant light exploded near his bed.

He was terrified and ran around behind his desk to hide. He couldn't see anything other than the light, and he called out to it, "Who are You?"

"I am the One you wanted to meet."

Instantly, the light was gone and a man stood in front of Ravi. It was the risen Christ Jesus. Ravi approached him, and he couldn't stop staring at his Lord's eyes. He told me He has the most beautiful eyes you have ever seen. When I asked him to describe what Jesus looks like, he paused for a moment, then said "He is dripping glory." It actually drips from Him. Ravi touched Jesus, and He was as real as I am. They sat in his room and spoke for hours, and the Lord told him many things and gave him many assignments. Ravi's roommates were in the living room, and they could even hear Ravi speaking to someone, and the man responding to him. They asked him later who the man with the deep voice was. Imagine their surprise when they found out who it had been!

A few days later, his fast was over. It was February 14, Valentine's Day. A woman he had been pursuing with little success called him out of the blue and told him she wanted to spend the rest of her life with him. He had asked her many times to marry him, but she had always said no. This time, she said yes. The Lord had made good on Ravi's request after all.

RIDING SHOTGUN

The second time the Lord appeared to Ravi revealed the more humorous side of God. Ravi had just dropped off his fiancée at her apartment, and she asked Ravi if he thought Jesus would ever appear to him again. He said no, he didn't think He would. He had done it once and that was enough.

As Ravi was pulling away from her apartment complex and onto the highway, Jesus instantly appeared in the seat next to him. The shock of it almost scared Ravi to death, and he jumped and yelled, "Don't do that! You have to give me some warning before You do that!" As soon as he said it, he realized Who he was talking to, and how he had just spoken to Him. But Jesus, the God of the universe, just smiled at him and said, "Sorry." Ravi's heart melted. The King of kings had just said sorry to him. How much more humbling could it get?

Jesus once again began talking to Ravi about certain things and events that were going to happen, particular people he was going to meet, and what exactly he was supposed to say to them when he did meet them. Ravi was so intent on listening that he didn't pay attention to his driving, and he soon saw flashing lights in his rearview mirror. Jesus Christ was riding shotgun, and he had just been pulled over by a cop.

Ravi put the car in park, and the officer looked up his license plate behind him. Jesus finished what He was saying to Ravi, then disappeared. The officer soon approached the car and tapped on the window. He asked for Ravi's license and registration, then asked the question Ravi was dreading.

"Where did the man go who was sitting next to you?"

Ravi looked at the empty seat.

"What man?"

"The one wearing the white shirt. He was in here when I pulled you over. Where did he go?"

Ravi looked again at the empty seat.

"He's not here anymore."

"Well who was he?"

This was it. Ravi had no choice but to tell the truth.

"He was Jesus Christ in the flesh."

The cop stared at him, then stood up for a second. Ravi had no idea what he was doing, but he quickly bent over again, handed Ravi his license and registration back, and told him to have a nice night and drive more carefully next time.

That's one of my all time favorite Ravi stories, because it reminds me that the God I am deeply in love with has an amazing sense of timing, as well as an unparalleled sense of humor.

TRUSTING GOD

Ravi has told me many, many stories of miraculous events that happened to him. Perhaps one day I will be allowed to share them all with you. But in spending time with him, and with others like him around the world, people who have completely sold out to God in a way that both challenges me and puts me to shame, the same basic truth rises to the surface. All of these people, no matter who they are or where they come from, *trust God*. They may struggle with Him, disagree with Him, get angry at Him, complain to Him, whine to Him, and sometimes even yell at Him; but in the end, they bow to His will because they trust that He has their best interests at heart, and that He loves them more than they love Him. How can you not trust someone like that?

Trusting God is a necessity as a Christian. But often that trust must be hard earned. God will not make things easy for us, because true love must withstand tests. God is looking for a people who will trust Him with everything, and not *just* believe in Him. Believing that I'm married to my wife and trusting her are two very different things. The whole situation gets marred and distorted, though, when we have so often been failed by others. We have been hurt by people who claim to know God, who claim to love Him, and who claim to be doing His will even as they hurt us.

But God is not asking us to put blind faith in men and women; He is asking us to *put trusting faith in Him* and Him alone. It is easy for Christians to believe in their minds that God loves them and cares about what they care about, but it is a little more difficult to fully entrust their lives to Him when, for many, they feel like they don't even know who He is. The only example of Christ they have seen is fallen people who maybe don't make the best representatives of who Christ is and how He sees you.

This is the reason, I think, that God decided to write a book. The Bible is His autobiography, and it is His love letter to all of us.

Chapter 13

THE NEW MODEL

When I began this journey, I was a skeptic. It's been well-documented and I'm not afraid to talk about it. I had no overriding motivation to prove to the world that God is a God of miracles or that everyone needs to believe that gold teeth are from Him. I didn't set out to try to get every church to become more Charismatic. I didn't even start out wanting to show that the Gospel is ultimately about love (after all, I thought it was mainly about getting people to sign on the dotted line of salvation so they'd receive their "get out of hell free" card).

Faith was supposed to be normal, quiet, unobtrusive, and meek. It was mostly intended to find form within the walls of a church building, God's house. We were God's children, and as His children, we were supposed to live upright, moral lives. We were supposed to be nice people. Respectful. Hopefully our behavior would show others that God was real, but in reality, me being a good boy simply let other people know that I wouldn't do bad things. I was a Christian, and they would know that, and we'd all coexist just fine as long as I didn't start turning into a religious freak or a zealot. That was actually one of my greatest fears while in my 20s. I didn't want anyone to think I was any different from them. It would "ruin my witness" because it would mean I was different from them on some level.

In reality, my constant striving to be the same as the rest of the world didn't allow me a better opportunity to present the Gospel to them, because even though I could, I never did. My faith was a sham built upon ideals and upbringing, with the occasional "God moments" thrown in for a little spice and to allow me to think that I was legit.

But my belief in God was just that—belief. It never ventured into a real relationship because, as I mentioned earlier, I couldn't trust God. I knew He loved me, but I had a sneaking suspicion that He didn't like me very much. After all, He knew my heart, He knew my innermost thoughts. He saw what I did when no one was looking. He could read my mind. How could He like me? How was that even possible? I felt like He loved me because He had to, like it was some obligation based on the contract He had written through Jesus' sacrifice. His love for me was obligatory, but not by choice.

I had said the magic words, probably more out of fear than anything else, but I had said them nonetheless, and that meant I was in His club. I had joined His family. I certainly wasn't His favorite kid, not by a long shot. There were other children who were doing far greater things for Him than I was, people who had sold out to His will and had made so many sacrifices that I was very much not willing to do myself.

No, I was going to live my life like a normal person, try to be successful at what I do, try to be as nice of a person as I could be, try to stay out of trouble, and, well, try to be happy. That was where I stood. And that's where I would have stayed had my wife not talked me into asking Him for an idea on a cold night in December 2005.

THE REAL GOD

My primary motivation for being a skeptic in the first place was that I didn't want to be duped into believing something that wasn't true. I wanted to believe in the real God, have solid, airtight theology, and above all, I wanted to make certain that I understood what I believed and why I believed it. I watched as my family started believing strange things, weird stories, and sheer impossibilities, but I also watched as, one by one, they were radically touched by a God who didn't seem mad or upset with them at all, but instead (could it be?) chose to love them despite their limitations. I couldn't deny that my family, smart people every one of them, were being changed for the better.

But how was I supposed to believe the stories they were telling me? People being raised from the dead? Gold teeth? Limbs growing back instantly? When I heard this stuff, I was instantly defensive. It didn't make sense. It wasn't tidy. It wasn't neat. True, there was weird stuff like this in the Bible, and yes, the stories I read in the Bible were even *stranger* than the ones I was hearing now, but come on, this is the 21st century. Most people just sit at home and watch television now. Life is normal. There's no need for the extreme anymore.

I think the biggest hurdle I had to overcome was dealing with the many scam artists who have come and gone. I think when you get right down to it, people are just sick and tired of being taken advantage of. We've maybe stepped out in belief in the past, but then we got burned. Maybe we started checking out what was happening with that dude with the tattoos down in Florida, but then his marriage dissolved and the whole thing fell down like a house of cards. Maybe we actually went forward at church for prayer once, and nothing happened, just as we feared. Maybe we went to that church people kept talking about, and maybe everyone there was so strange that we vowed never to make that mistake again. Maybe we've just seen enough televangelists hawking phony merchandise telling us it's holy and anointed, and that if we just send a little money, God will grant us our wish. Maybe… the list can go on, can't it? Mine sure could.

The truth is, I just figured it was easier and safer to stick with the basics, do church the way it's always been done, and keep my head out of the line of fire. Imagine, though, if that is what the disciples had done? Or the early church? Or the Christians in China? Or Heidi Baker? The places around the world where Christianity is growing at a rapid rate are the very places that embrace what God wants to do through radical people who want only His presence and a relationship with Him.

My problem, for a very long time, was that I had gotten too sophisticated. I had honed my belief in God into a tidy box, and I kept the things that I liked and rejected the things that I didn't. I was only comfortable with a God I could fully understand. So I built my understanding around what I found acceptable. What I found acceptable was limited to what I had seen for myself. What I had seen for myself was…well…

it was church as church. It was four songs, announcements, send the kids to Sunday school, tithe, sermon, one more song, and then head home to watch football. That was what I had reduced the God of the universe to.

HE HAS HIS REASONS

Jesus said that you can only inherit the Kingdom of God if you become like a child. He's not talking about sucking your thumb or playing with toy trucks, He's talking about a mindset. When I look at my own children, I see my own failures. They aren't sophisticated. They can't even spell the word. Their Jesus can do whatever He wants to do, and yes, He hears them when they pray to Him. If He doesn't answer their prayer for something specific, they just ask again. They don't have any major crisis of faith because God is God; He obviously knows best. When they watch their daddy's movie, they think the gemstones are so cool. Of course God can do that if He wants to. It doesn't get them all bent out of shape because they can't figure out *why* He did it. He's God; He obviously has His reasons.

Why can't I have faith like this? I've seen so much over the past few years, more than most people probably. Yet why do I still suffer pangs of doubt over some of the things I see and hear?

Maybe because I've seen the other side as well. I've seen the crowds looking to a *person* for healing instead of to *God*. I've seen ministers working a crowd into a frenzy to the point that their minds switch off and they just go with the flow of everyone else. I've seen friends of mine, people I trust, get carried away and play to the emotions of a crowd. I've seen them stretch the truth. I've heard their stories change a little to suit their audience. And of course, I watch the news. I've seen the big guys fall. I've watched as hidden sins leap to the surface and destroy credibility. I've read about the scam artists planting gemstones in sanctuaries beforehand. I've talked with people who are obviously mentally off-kilter. In truth, I've seen exactly what I feared I would see.

But I've seen more than that too. I've seen humble men and women, all around the world, who don't even want me to film them because they don't want to draw attention to themselves. I've seen miracles happen in front of my eyes. I've looked into the eyes of someone who was just healed and have seen the overwhelming joy and disbelief that this actually happened to them, of all people. I've seen ministries that exist with very little support, and I've met missionaries who are loathe to ask anyone for anything, lest they be lumped in with the scam artists. I've met countless people who simply want to let God do all the work, and in turn, get all the glory.

IN THE END

In the end, the only person I can be accountable for is myself. It's hard for me to judge people anymore, simply because I see myself in all of them. I see my own ambition in that evangelist onstage, and I see my own humble adoration of what God can do through a broken vessel in that child praying for another child in the dirt. I am the best of what I see, and I am the worst of what I see. And I am reminded that, in the end, none of this is about me anyway. It is about my King.

I used to use stupid Christians as an excuse not to open up my life to the true power of God. But that was just an excuse, because I'm just as stupid as anyone. I used to hide behind the mistakes of men and women, the so-called spokespeople for God, as a reason to keep my head low and live a normal life. But I ignored my own mistakes, my own faults, my own frailties. I had an excuse for every argument you could throw my way; and if I really thought about it, I wouldn't even be able to tell you why I was arguing with you. I guess I just wanted to stay within the status quo. I just wanted to live my life and be normal. I didn't want to be challenged. I didn't want more expected of me. I didn't want to talk to strangers. I didn't want to give up control.

A NEW DAY

But today is a new day. In the past, I thought the church existed for believers. I thought it was a repository for fellow Christians to come together and worship, hear sermons, and get ready for the week ahead in the "real world." I used to think the church was a building. If it was a community, it was a fractured one. If it was a family, it was a dysfunctional one. There might be 40 churches in a town, and they all pretty much stayed out of each others' way. You do your thing, we'll do ours, and I guess we'll meet up in Heaven.

It seems to me, while traveling the world and getting a taste of what is happening as well as what is possible, that the Western church, for the most part, has a local focus. We worry about our community because that's how we'll grow. The church too often is a place designed to perpetuate its own survival, and all of its focus and intentions point toward that belief.

I have seen some of the best that God's kids have to offer the world—I've seen churches that are alive and bursting with the Gospel, and in each place there is a focus that goes way beyond just what their church is interested in. It is a focus, a near obsession, in fact, with the Kingdom of God. This is the same Kingdom Jesus preached over and over again—it was His obsession as well. When He said, *"the Kingdom of God has come upon you"* (Matt. 12:28), I don't think he really meant to say that "the church of God is upon you." The church is incredibly important, and it certainly shouldn't go away, but its focus must change if the Gospel of Jesus Christ is going to spill out of its doors into the streets where the hurting and the hungry live.

The Kingdom of God is a place of unity. It is "other" focused. It is motivated entirely by love and compassion, not by pity or guilt. His Kingdom is not interested in controlling people or God. It simply makes itself available, free of obligation. It is not motivated by the number of people who walk through the door. Of course, I have also observed that wherever God is allowed to really move, and when His Kingdom is at the center of everything and the Holy Spirit is the Guide, growth is usually explosive. People around the world, in every culture, respond to the same thing—love.

The world is tired of being judged, but it is waiting, longing, hoping, to be *loved*. It is time we begin putting on our makeup as the Bride of Christ. It is time we start making ourselves beautiful to Him again. If our beauty is found in love, are we ready for our makeover?

So go ahead, ask Him for an idea.

I dare you.

Darren Wilson is founder/CEO of Wanderlust Productions in Chicago, Illinois. Wanderlust is a film/television production company dedicated to advancing the Kingdom of God through creative and entertaining media. For most of his life, Darren was a believing but skeptical Christian. A college professor, he prided himself on rationally understanding God's love and activity in the world today. In May 2006, Darren had an angelic visitation from an angel named Breakthrough that set him on course to make his first feature film, *Finger of God*.

Finger of God details Darren's very personal journey around the world chasing after the miraculous, trying to see if God was actually doing some of the things Darren had been hearing about but simply could not believe. Made on a shoestring budget of $20,000 and borrowed equipment, *Finger of God* went on to sell over 70,000 copies without any advertising and has been seen and embraced by millions worldwide.

Darren followed up with *Furious Love,* a sequel of sorts to *Finger of God.* In *Furious Love,* Darren once again travels the world, but this time he is trying to answer the question of whether or not there are any limits to God's love. Darren and his crew travel to some of the darkest spiritual climates on the planet: the sex trade in Thailand, the persecuted church in India, heroin addicts in Madrid, New Age and Witchcraft festivals, and many more. The result is a haunting film that many are calling the most powerful movie they have ever seen. *Furious Love* was released in churches on Valentine's Day 2010, and has been shown in over 1,000 churches worldwide.

Darren is currently working on a number of projects, including a cartoon series, a film about Ultimate Fighting Championship legend Ken Shamrock, and the third film in the *Finger/Furious* trilogy, entitled *Father of Lights*.

Darren is also the Artist-in-Residence at Judson University in Elgin, Illinois, and heads up the Wanderlust Foundation, a non-profit organization dedicated to training students in advanced media techniques and bringing awareness to various ministries worldwide.

Darren and his wife, Jenell, live near Chicago, Illinois, with their three children, Serenity, Stryder, and River.

For more information about Darren, his movies, or his production company, please contact:

Wanderlust Productions
1151 N. State Street
Elgin, IL 60123
Studio Phone: 847-628-1142

Fax: 847-628-1143
Website: www.wanderlustproductions.net
Email: contact@wanderlustproductions.net

In the right hands, This Book will Change Lives!

Most of the people who need this message will not be looking for this book. To change their lives, you need to put a copy of this book in their hands.

> *But others (seeds) fell into good ground, and brought forth fruit, some a hundred-fold, some sixty-fold, some thirty-fold* (Matthew 13:8).

Our ministry is constantly seeking methods to find the good ground, the people who need this anointed message to change their lives. Will you help us reach these people?

> *Remember this—a farmer who plants only a few seeds will get a small crop. But the one who plants generously will get a generous crop* (2 Corinthians 9:6).

EXTEND THIS MINISTRY BY SOWING
3 BOOKS, 5 BOOKS, 10 BOOKS, OR MORE TODAY,
AND BECOME A LIFE CHANGER!

Thank you,

Don Nori Sr., Publisher
Destiny Image
Since 1982

DESTINY IMAGE PUBLISHERS, INC.

*"Speaking to the Purposes of God for This Generation
and for the Generations to Come."*

VISIT OUR NEW SITE HOME AT
WWW.DESTINYIMAGE.COM

FREE SUBSCRIPTION TO DI NEWSLETTER

Receive free unpublished articles by top DI authors, exclusive

discounts, and free downloads from our best and newest books.

Visit www.destinyimage.com to subscribe.

Write to: Destiny Image
             P.O. Box 310
             Shippensburg, PA 17257-0310

Call: 1-800-722-6774

Email: orders@destinyimage.com

For a complete list of our titles or to place an order
online, visit www.destinyimage.com.

FIND US ON FACEBOOK OR FOLLOW US ON TWITTER.

www.facebook.com/destinyimage   facebook
www.twitter.com/destinyimage   twitter